SPANIELS

SPANIELS

Gerald Bishop

David & Charles
Newton Abbot   London   North Pomfret (Vt)

British Library Cataloguing in Publication Data

Bishop, Gerald
  Spaniels
  1. Spaniels
  I. Title
  636.7'52   SF429.S7

ISBN 0-7153-8483-X

Typeset by Typesetters (Birmingham) Ltd
and printed in Great Britain by
Butler & Tanner Ltd Frome and London
for David & Charles (Publishers) Limited
Brunel House Newton Abbot Devon

Published in the United States of America
by David & Charles Inc
North Pomfret Vermont 05053 USA

Contents

	Preface	7
1	From Dog to Spaniel	9
2	Spaniel Breeds and Personalities	16
3	Choosing a Spaniel	56
4	Puppy Care	64
5	Breeding	73
6	Feeding	83
7	Handling and Grooming	88
8	Exercise and General Training	102
9	Showing and the Breed Standards	115
10	The Working Spaniel	145
11	Emergencies and First Aid	152
12	Medical Care, Disorders and Illnesses	163
	Appendices:	
	1 Parts and Points of the Dog	179
	2 Quarantine	182
	3 Useful Addresses	183
	Acknowledgements	189
	Index	190

To my spaniels, past and present, who have inspired me to write, and to all the dogs whose lives I have been privileged to share. To Gipsy and Joanna, who are the finest companions and very much alive, to Khan, a crazy but lovable Afghan Hound, whose life sadly ended while this book was being written, and to the fond memories of Judy, Chloe and Bruce in particular.

Preface

This book covers all members of that branch of the dog 'family' known as 'spaniels'. There are not enough books devoted to this group of dog breeds, which in my opinion offers man the highest devotion, the finest loyalty and the closest unquestioning companionship given by any dog since those far-off days when the first wild dogs inveigled themselves into the camps of early tribes.

Included here are fifteen breeds of spaniel – from the tiny Papillon (or Butterfly Spaniel) and the small, alert Tibetan, to the faithful 'merry' Cocker, the loyal, jolly Welsh Springer and the heavy, dignified Clumber. The eager, clowning nature of the Irish Water is described, the unique beauty of the Sussex, the gentleness of the Field, and the strength of character of the English Springer, the differences between the soft, aristocratic virtues of the King Charles and the adaptable, friendly Cavalier King Charles. The Brittany, with its value as a working dog and companion, is also included, and there are descriptions of the American Cocker (now often bred in Britain) and the American Water as well as the American version of the English Springer. All breeds are fine, loyal and intelligent companions, but each is an individual with its own special qualities.

This book aims to provide firstly an introduction to an outstanding sector of the canine community, secondly some insight into individual personalities and needs, and thirdly some guidelines on care and management of spaniels, and on enhancing the companionship between dog and owner by means of a sound understanding.

It would be unfair, even in a work of this kind, to omit to embrace the entire dog species in a gesture of affection and gratitude. When I was a boy, and my dearest friend – a small black Cocker Spaniel – finally died, I shed many tears at her memory, and an old man who knew both of us said: 'While you loved *that* dog, it is really *the* dog you love and you will

7

have many more to follow her and each of them will have a place in your life and in your heart.' He was right, and nearly forty years later, all dogs I had and still have as companions keep their individual places. We owe perhaps the greatest debt of gratitude to the dog, which is the only 'domestic' animal whose companionship to man has not been forced upon it. And yet I find it hard to mention this debt without remembering the millions of dogs that die or suffer by man's hand every year. Those that have good homes and human companions who care about them, repaying in small measure the extremes of loyalty and devotion that most dogs give, are the lucky ones. In this book, though I have remembered just a few of the happy breed of spaniels, it is really 'the dog' that earns the tributes.

If this book helps to match the right human to the right dog, adds a little to that human's knowledge of the dog's needs and welfare, and starts a reciprocal friendship that lasts the dog's lifetime, I have achieved my aim; that spaniels as yet unborn may benefit.

1

From Dog to Spaniel

The spaniel is a remarkable dog, resembling no other breed in disposition and personality. Centuries ago a writer referred to the 'merry spaniel', and this aspect of its nature, coupled with its loyalty and intelligence, makes it an attractive animal indeed. As a companion I have found none better.

The companionship of dog with man goes back to around 10,000BC. It probably evolved in various parts of the world in different circumstances, around the same time. The reasons for the dog's domestication was its common interest with man – hunting. Today there are over ninety pure breeds of dog, and spaniels have emerged as a special 'family' in a group that includes other scent-hunting, sporting dogs such as setters (a close relation, sometimes called 'setting spaniels'), retrievers and pointers. The ancestry of this group probably goes back to a line of mountain wolves. Taking the group into a broader section of the canine community, it is thought that the Tibetan wolf (*Canis lupus chanco*) is the most likely ancestor of what is called the 'mastiff group'; this includes, with mastiffs, the spaniels and their sporting companions mentioned above. It also includes the larger breed of 'soft' dogs – the Newfoundland, the St Bernard and the Pyrenean mountain dog.

The history of the spaniel, as of dogs in general, is confused, but it was probably around in several European countries, in one form or another, by the beginning of the twelfth century. One of the earliest written references to it comes from Geoffrey Chaucer (1340–1400): in his *Canterbury Tales*, the Prologue to the 'Wife of Bathe's Tale' comments: 'For as a spaynel she wol on hom lepe.' Shakespeare mentions the spaniel in *King Lear* (Act III, scene 6): 'Mastiff, grey-hound, mongrel grim, hound or spaniel, brach or lym'. In 1387 Gaston de Foix titled a chapter of his *Miroir de Phebus* 'Of spaniels and of their Nature', observing that 'They love well their masters and follow them without losing although they be in a great crowd of men.' He refers to their origin: 'Their kind cometh from Spain notwithstanding that there are many in other countries.'

Probably the earliest work in which dogs were mentioned in detail in English was a fourteenth-century manuscript titled *Maystre of Game* (largely a translation of *Livre de Chasse* by the French writer Gaston de Foix). It was written by Edward Duke of York, grandson of Edward III and master of game and hawk for part of his life to Henry IV. It was primarily devoted to hunting information and game, with dogs and their part in the sport being mentioned throughout, including the spaniel which York positively claims originated in Spain.

The earliest printed dog book was one on hawking and hunting by Dame Juliana Berners, born around 1388, who was Prioress of Sopwell Nunnery near St Albans in Hertfordshire. In discussing 'houndes' she also mentioned the 'spanyel'. Following her book, there were few major references to spaniels until Dr John Caius, physician to Queen Elizabeth I, prepared a relatively short work on English dogs in 1576. Dr Caius grouped the English dog breeds into three, and in one of these, 'a gentle kind serving game', he had a further classification, the 'Aucupatorii' – dogs used for fowling. These breeds were again divided, this time into two groups: the first was known as the 'Index' or 'Setter' and the other the 'Aquaticus' or 'Spaniel'. He also mentioned the 'spaniel gentle' or 'comforter' – a name to be carried forward for many years and referring to the King Charles types of spaniel. These dogs he grouped separately, describing them as a 'currish kind, meet for many toyes'. Between Dame Juliana Berners' time and that of Dr Caius the number of dog breeds around appears to have substantially increased – and the spaniel is mentioned in each work. It seems to have been around and recognised – especially as a working dog – since the early fourteenth century.

In 1575 a *Booke of Faulconrie* by George Tumberville remarked 'howe necessary a thing a spanell is to Faulconrie'. Almost a hundred years later, in his *Diary* of 8 July 1647, John Evelyn wrote: 'I lost my faithful spaniel Piccoli who had followed me from Rome, it seems he had been taken up by

Early woodcut illustrations of spaniels

some of the Governor's pages or footmen without recovery, which was a great displeasure to me.'

The naturalist Linnaeus (1707–78) listed in his animal classification some thirty-six breeds of dog. Spaniels were given two categories – *Canis extrarius* and *Canis hyspanicus*. The French naturalist Georges Cuvier (1769–1832) divided the canine world into three groups, identifying them by various anatomical features. The first of the three groups, 'matins', were dogs with a fairly elongated head, the parietal or side bones drawn towards each other. This classification included the Scotch, Irish and Italian greyhounds, the boar-hound, the dingo (or 'New Holland Dog'), the molossus (mastiff), the Danish dog and the lesser Danish dog (now known as the dalmatian).

The second of Cuvier's canine groups, the 'dogues', were those with somewhat shortened muzzles, high skulls with considerable frontal sinuses and the lower jaw extending below the upper. Rather surprisingly, Cuvier includes the mastiff in this section, along with the bulldog.

The third group was more specific and named 'spaniels'. These were described as having a head only moderately elongated, the parietal bones not approaching each other but swelling out to enlarge the cerebral cavity – perhaps inferring a superior intelligence! In this group Cuvier mentioned the 'Alpine Spaniels', which were almost certainly the lemon-and-white forefathers of the present Clumber Spaniel, referred to as being similar to Newfoundlands and again mastiffs – and additionally probably the St Bernard. Also listed with this group were the 'hound', the sheepdog and the wolfhound.

In terms of the breeds around today, some of Cuvier's classification remains confusing (especially as the mastiff appeared in all three groups in one form or another). No mention was made of setters or pointers – often grouped with spaniels in other works. The 'Alpine' breeds, however, seem to have given their name (and probably some ancestry) to some of the present-day spaniel breeds – that is if Cuvier's classification is at least partly accepted.

Dr Caius, writing in earlier times than Cuvier, referred to spaniels in some detail and divided them into two groups – those that 'findeth game on the land' and those that 'findeth game on the water'. These tasks were done with the aid of the hawk and the net.

> The common sort of people call them by one general word, namely Spaniells. As though these kinde of Dogges came originally and first of all out of Spaine. The most part of their skynnes are white, and if they are marcked with any spottes, they are commonly red, and somewhat great therewithall, the heares not growing in such thicknesse but that the mixture of them maye easely be perceaved.

'Othersome of them be reddishe and blackishe, but of that sorte there be but a few', he said, and referred to 'a newe kinde of dogge brought out of Fraunce . . . they bee speckled all ouer with white and black, which colours incline to a marble blewe, which bewtifyeth their skinnes and affordeth a seemely show of comlynesse.' This latter description could well fit a blue-roan spaniel, and Dr Caius appears to have been in doubt about the number of spaniel breeds. Almost certainly there were several (he even mentions the Water Spaniel as another breed, elsewhere in his book), and it is evident that many of the colour variations we know today had already arrived. Back in 1697, the author of the *Gentleman's Recreation*, Nicholas Cox, also applauded the spaniel as a working dog. He had evident knowledge of the breed, referring to it as being used for both springing and retrieving, and stated that it could be trained as a setting dog, alluding to the assumption that the setter has developed from the spaniel. He described the spaniel as 'being of a good and nimble size, rather small than gross, and of a courageous mettle . . . lusty and nimble rangers, of active feet, wanton tails and busie nostrils' – not a bad description of the cheerful spaniel nature! Cox adds that the spaniel's 'tail was without weariness, their search without changeableness, and whom no delight did transport beyond fear of obedience' – a delightful description of some of the spaniel's real characteristics. Samuel Pepys (1633–1703) often referred in his diaries to the King with a train of spaniels in St James' Park.

In *Cynographia Britannica*, written in 1801 by Sydenham

Edwards, a colour plate shows four dogs – a black-and-white, a liver-and-white, an orange-and-white, and a sandy liver. Spaniels are simply divided into land and water spaniels, with the land breeds comprising the springing, hawking spaniel – or 'starter' – and the 'cocking spaniel' – or Cocker. Apparently he felt there were few of the springing variety around, except in London. The Cocker is described as having a round head, compact form, short nose, long ears, short, strong limbs and a coat more inclined to curl than the Springer's. Colours around then appeared to be liver-and-white, red, red-and-white, black-and-white, all liver and 'sometimes black with tanned legs and muzzle'. At that time spaniels, as 'starters', were working with greyhounds to hunt hares as well as birds. Their coats are described by Edwards as 'beautiful'; their dispositions 'faithful'; their manners 'humble and insinuating', with 'sauvity' and 'obedience even to servility' procuring them 'universal favour'. That favour has followed them through several centuries.

In the *Sportsman's Cabinet* in 1803, W. Taplin refers to the 'large Springing Spaniel and the diminutive Cocker', but in 1814 William Dobson of Eden Hall, Cumberland, published a work on the training of 'Pointers and Spaniels', generally assuming, it seems, that the spaniel and the setter were one and the same breed. Cassell's *Popular Natural History*, published in the mid-nineteenth century, often refers to the intelligence of the spaniel, and illustrations show the breed in various forms. The Cocker is described as 'the smallest of the land spaniels', chiefly used in flushing woodcock and pheasant in thickets and copses, 'into which the setter and springer can scarcely enter'.

The Blenheim Spaniel (the ancestor of the King Charles and the Cavalier) has been reared by one of the Dukes of Marlborough; 'from its beauty and gaiety, it is more frequently found in the drawing room than the field; but it occasionally breaks out and shows what it is prepared to do.' Accurate descriptions of these two different breeds!

The 'Water Spaniel' is referred to as 'generally liver-coloured and white, with the hair of the body crisped, or disposed in little knots', moderate in size, strong, active, and intelligent, and of great service to the water-fowl shooter,

14

either along the sea-coast, or amidst fens and marshes. This is a good illustration of today's Irish Water Spaniel. The 'rough water dog', was also a 'most intelligent and valuable animal' – another curly-coated dog, it seems. In the same context the French 'Barbet' is mentioned – a forerunner of the poodle rather than the spaniels, though often confused with them.

The spaniel's qualities, its merry, loyal and affectionate nature, and its outstanding personality, have assured it a place with man for all time, as a fine companion and a good working dog. In all its forms it is worthy of respect, and in return for its loyalty each owner bears responsibility for its welfare and preservation. This does not only mean that the spaniel's lineage should be perpetuated – luckily some responsible breeders are seeing to that, and not just for financial gain, for there are no millions to be made from breeding dogs in the proper way. But if you take on a spaniel, you make a commitment for the whole of its life. That gorgeous new puppy is not a toy; it will chew – prized possessions too, if you are not careful enough – and mess and wet around the house, cry and bark; it cannot be disposed of when the family realise that it needs to be trained, as a child needs to be taught, that it needs comfort and companionship, understanding and, above all, love and attention. It costs money to keep, and it needs patience to understand. But if you can give all that . . . you'll have a happy partnership.

2

Spaniel Breeds
and Personalities

There was no definite time in history when the spaniel as we know it stepped out of the shrubbery wagging its tail and talking among its audience. It has been with us for a long time as a distinct race, a dog among dogs and a dog among men. And the several breeds of spaniel vary in style, personality and looks. Though they are all – in my view correctly – known as spaniels, they are indeed very different. The various breeds have gradually acquired Kennel Club 'standards' of their own, so that the 'ideal' strain of each can be kept pure, and a line of the best blood can be followed in each one in the future.

In Victorian times, when for the more fortunate classes leisure was more than just a pastime, exhibitions and entertainments aiming to add to people's knowledge were in fashion. The Great Exhibition of 1851 set the trend for many shows in years to come, and in some of these dogs were included. The new railways enabled visitors, exhibitors and dogs to travel all over the country, and the 'dog show' began to popularise (and standardise) different breeds. Gentlemen's working dogs were much talked about, and while the first organised dog show was held in 1859 at Newcastle-upon-Tyne, various gundog trials were in the making. What were probably the first trials for the Cocker Spaniel, for example, were held in 1899 at Sutton Scarsdale and promoted by William Arkwright, who incidentally bred a well-known Clumber Spaniel called Lapis in 1875. These trials demonstrated the Cocker's talents as a working gundog.

The Kennel Club was founded in 1873, and one of its first tasks was the compilation of a Stud Book, the first volume containing records of shows from 1859. Ten simple rules governed future dog shows then, with winners eligible for entry in the Stud Book – which has appeared each year since.

16

More rules and regulations were added later. One of the milestones of the Kennel Club was the movement to stop the cropping of dogs' ears, supported fervently by the Prince of Wales: since April 1898, dogs with cropped ears have been ineligible for competitions under Kennel Club rules. Today the Kennel Club registers an average of 200,000 dogs a year and has become more closely involved with somewhat wider aspects of dog ownership; but the Club's main objective is still to improve pure-bred dogs.

Under Kennel Club regulations, spaniels are generally classified within the Gundog Group, which includes pointers, setters and retrievers as well. In this group are listed Cocker, Clumber, Brittany, English and Welsh Springer, Sussex, Field, Irish Water and American Cocker Spaniels. Tibetan Spaniels are classified as members of the Utility Group, along with dalmations, schnauzers, poodles and others. King Charles, Papillons and Cavalier King Charles are classified as Toy Dogs, with griffons, pugs, Yorkshire terriers, etc. The other groups are Terrier, Hound and Working – the latter including alsatians, mastiffs, collies, great danes, corgis and others.

With standards being formulated and the working and show dogs becoming much in evidence at the turn of the century, so the breeds of spaniel we know today began to appear in definite form. Those that had stood the test of time were to continue, with the 'best' features of each breed being passed down from one 'ideal' standard couple to the next generation. Other less-established breeds were to become more standardised, with better features encouraged and faults gradually eliminated through careful breeding programmes by responsible breeders conforming to authoritative descriptions. Some breeds, sadly, became extinct by this method, for publicity adds strength to brand or breed, and less popular dogs without strong human champions would slowly disappear. A few breeds tottering on the brink of extinction were rescued, to survive and appear in today's breed lists.

I have known all spaniel breeds, and the Cocker is my current favourite. But as the spaniel breeds differ, so do people's preferences, and your choice will depend on which

17

spaniel best fits your own personality and lifestyle. Matching humans and dogs can be a tricky process – although if you love dogs, it is true that in the final analysis almost any intelligent dog will do. My own love for the Cocker may go back to the fact that a little black Cocker bitch puppy was given to be by my parents when I was eight years old. I loved dogs (as indeed most animals) and Judy gave me a special attachment for the breed; I vowed that she would be the first of many. She was, but like all the others since, she was an individual with a special personality of her own, and good qualities which I have discovered are common to all breeds of spaniel. Judy was with me throughout my childhood and we could never wait for the holidays and weekends when we would roam hedgerows and fields on our special long country walks. She would sit by my side while I rummaged in holes in the ground or poked around with net and jam-jar in ponds. Just being with me was enough and the bond between us was never broken.

This firm attachment may have been made stronger by the fact that she went blind when quite young and although my father spent much time and money trying to have her cured, nothing could be done. She was always happy, though, and her senses of hearing and smell became much more acute due to her blindness. My father made her a sort of crash helmet – an adapted muzzle with the front cut away and reversed so that it would fit over her head and project out as a shield for her eyes. The furniture at home was kept pretty well in place and, when she entered a room, Judy would slowly follow the wall round, touching herself round the furniture with her shoulder or her crash helmet.

She was always jolly, wagging her tail continuously. When released from her lead in a field or wood for her run, she would follow her nose, charging around scenting the breeze and listening for my whistle which would either warn her of an object in her way or bring her back to me. Her training was important to her of course and she was obedient as a result. In woodland she would progress more slowly but would often chase rabbits and veer off from a tree with the speed and accuracy of an experienced racing driver when she detected the telltale rise of the roots in the ground. She rarely hurt herself and her life was a constant reminder to me that the decision to let her live it out was the right one to make.

The Cocker

The Cocker Spaniel, a devoted companion offering loyalty, intelligence and a loving nature, with a merry disposition, has never been in danger of dying out. Its history can be traced back to the fourteenth century, and it seems to be more or less unchanged in temperament, according to chroniclers through the years. Before 1880 'field' spaniels, as they were by then generally termed, were divided into two groups. The lighter of the two was more successful – and perhaps more cautious – at flushing woodcock and became known as the 'Cocker' or 'Cocking' Spaniel. The heavier larger version of the same breed was used for 'springing' game and was called the 'Springer' or 'Springing' Spaniel.

The Cocker has always been applauded for its quick intelligence and eagerness to please. Even its silvery-toned voice when working has added to its popularity. As with every

Two blue-roan Cocker Spaniels, Cutel Cobweb (right) and Cutel Cherubs Darling, owned by Mrs A. J. Quartermain

species individuals vary, but this dog is characteristically gentle in nature, extremely loyal, inquisitive and fond of well-deserved praise and attention.

The dog's height is about 39–41cm (15½–16in), and bitches about 38cm (15in). Sizes vary with the strain, some being quite small and delicate, others relatively stocky. Generally they weigh about 11–13kg (24–28lb).

Colours are black, blue-roan, black-and-white, red-and-white or golden. The coat is usually flat and silky, often with white on the chest, especially in the self colours.

Of the two blue-roan Cocker bitches I now own, one could be described as an introvert, the other as an extrovert; both are cheerful animals who rarely leave my side. The younger, Joanna, is the dominant one, a good house dog and when in the mood, full of harmless mischief. Gipsy, though with a less outgoing personality, has her own ways of countering Joanna's dominance, and they live and play happily together, only really competing with each other if one should dig up a bone or find some titbit the other has missed. Gipsy has always been interested in molehills, and on a walk will meticulously inspect these, or mouseholes, squirrel caches, and other small animal habitats. When Joanna first came on the scene as a puppy she found Gipsy's devotion to these crevices and crannies hard to take – especially in the middle of a game – and would bark to attract her attention away from the hole. At first Gipsy almost always responded, but later she realised it was a ruse to get her away from the hole. Nowadays, Joanna employs the same trick but uses a different bark – one which says in effect: 'What's this?' Gipsy lifts her head from the hole to see what it is all about and in goes Joanna's! They play the game regularly, and I can often see Gipsy peer out of the corner of her eye at Joanna in response to her bark. If she can see her, she will carry on digging, but if Joanna is outside her field of vision, she cannot resist lifting out her inquisitive nose.

Their personalities fit well with each other though probably their owner has been something of a catalyst. With Cocker Spaniels you can bring out the best in them by spending time with them, helping them develop and fitting into their own personalities. If a dog is dominant, for example, it only

Joanna and Gipsy, the author's Cocker Spaniel bitches

distresses it to make it submissive to other dogs. If it is nervous it will do no good to ignore it. Every dog's personality should be evaluated and allowances made for it – and Cockers are no exception. Handled correctly from puppyhood they are remarkably intelligent, very trusting, and can be guaranteed to cheer one out of the most doleful of moods.

The Springer – English and Welsh
Springer Spaniels are different – but equally lovable and reliable. There are two forms of Springer Spaniel around today; both have been in existence at least since the Middle Ages and both are pure breeds.

The English Springer Spaniel is similar to the Cocker in disposition – cheery and intelligent. It is a larger, strong, active dog with notable endurance. Other qualities include a fine loyalty and an easygoing temperament.

English Springer Spaniel Feorlig Quiller (owned by Mr & Mrs D. Miller) stands with true canine professionalism

Most usual colours are black-and-white and liver-and-white, but there are other colour variations around, including black, and often tan markings are present. The coat is close and straight, with a denseness suitable for weather-resistance. Both sexes are around 51cm (20in) in height, and longer in the leg than other land spaniels. Weight is about 23kg (50lb).

The Welsh Springer Spaniel is an ancient breed, a fine, loyal and jolly companion, well respected as a working dog, willing, faithful and active. It possesses great stamina and intelligence. It is equally at home working in water and on land.

The standard colour is a rich red-and-white, and the coat is straight or flat and thick, of a silky texture. Dogs are usually about 48cm (19in) in height and bitches around 46cm (18in). Weight is usually between 16 and 20kg (35 and 45lb).

English and Welsh Springer Spaniels are not dissimilar in appearance, though the former is somewhat heavier and altogether stockier in build. The English Springer seems to me to be more stolid in its outlook than its Welsh cousin, but is nonetheless a fine breed. Welsh Springer Spaniels perhaps are the closest to Cockers in mannerisms and merry nature. They too have remarkably good temperaments, are generally friendly towards each other when living together, and are extremely affectionate to those who make a fuss of them. For their owners Welsh Springers have much loyalty and an intelligence which is both keen and understanding. They need a good deal of exercise – not only for body conditioning, but also for retaining an alert mind. A country environment suits the active Welsh Springer, and shows its nature at its best.

The members of a family of Welsh Springers that I know (owned by Mr and Mrs J. S. Walton) are instantly recognisable by their individual characters. All have similar friendly, cheerful personalities but each one is different. As you enter their farmhouse home they all rush to welcome a visitor, each with his or her own form of greeting and every one hoping for a special response.

When a litter of puppies was born to one of the bitches, their own personalities started to emerge at a very early age; the two retained became integrated with the collective behaviour of the family. Of course the Welsh Springer varies, when specimens are chosen at random from various breeders and homes about the country (as do other spaniels), but this family collectively exhibit the special qualities of affection, intelligence and vitality common to good representatives of the breed.

The Welsh Springer's ancestry can, like the Cocker's, be traced back to the fourteenth century. It is likely that the Welsh and English Springers and Cockers were originally close in lineage, and were the first land spaniels. As already seen, the larger, stockier dogs which were best at springing game started the Springer breed and the smaller breed became known as Cockers. Some of the less attractive of today's

Cockers are too large and some Springers too small, which tends to support this theory.

It may not be a coincidence that while my favourite spaniel is the Cocker, the breed which comes close second is the Welsh Springer; their natures are similar, and they have a similar intelligence, loyalty and perception. Both have an extraordinary sense of fun and thoroughly enjoy involving others in their various forms of lively amusement.

A Welsh Springer Spaniel I once owned had always seen the need cheerfully to chase off cats – until my wife one day brought in a sad tortoiseshell cat who obviously needed a good understanding home. Bruce, the Springer, eyed Mitzi the cat with some amusement, wagging his tail and rear end mischieviously as he waited for the cat to run. Naturally we tried to train him to leave the cat in peace, but it was Mitzi herself who put the finishing touches to his education. When the urge was too much for him he would burst into a wild dash, chasing her up the nearest tree; but that first summer Mitzi eventually tired of the indignity of having to seek refuge from an unpredictable canine humorist. She sought a special position at the end of the garden when Bruce was around, ostentatiously sunning herself at the foot of a fence post. She would flaunt herself until the poor dog could withstand the temptation no longer, stalking her (a procedure which she pointedly ignored but of which she was well aware) and then playfully dashing at her. At the very last moment the cat would spring smartly to the top of the fence post and the dog, unable to stop in time, would crash headlong into the fence. After a few lessons of this nature he shook himself and retreated. They became good friends later, and although Bruce never lost his habit of chasing unknown cats, he did not again take off after Mitzi.

Perhaps he had his revenge in another way. For a short time we stayed with friends who had a young Labrador dog – and a cat. The Labrador was on good terms with the house cat but Bruce thought it was fair game, and despite some chastisement from me, insisted on chasing it around the

Polly, a fine Welsh Springer Spaniel (Hill Park Hippolyta, owned by Mr & Mrs J. S. Walton)

house – until it finally bolted through its cat door into the garden, leaving Bruce with his head pushed firmly through the cat door and the rest of him waving furiously inside the kitchen. The Labrador looked on. By the time we left, some two weeks later, Bruce had finally become obedient on the matter of chasing the cat and permanently ignored its presence. He had apparently fulfilled his mission however, since it was the Labrador who now chased the poor cat around the house and as far through the cat door as he could extend his head!

Springers, as well as being excellent companions, are extremely reliable working dogs, 'springing' and retrieving well in a variety of conditions. They are popular in the UK and various parts of Europe, especially the Netherlands, and in the USA – where the Welsh Springer is particularly liked.

Springer Spaniels were used in the Middle Ages, as we have seen, for springing game from cover for the human hunter to bring down with the aid of falcon or greyhound – depending on whether the quarry was furred or feathered. 'Welshies', as they are often called, were indeed bred in Wales, where they generally worked to spring game into a net.

Countless writers and dog historians have differently interpreted the dogs in old paintings, some from such great masters as Van Dyck or Gainsborough. The point is, surely, that the paintings were made some time later from quick sketches of a mobile creature. St Bernards, Newfoundlands or mastiffs are unmistakable anywhere, but some of the spaniel paintings could show any form of Cocker, Springer, Field, Sussex and so on; many of them were probably crossbred anyway. Unless the dog is as distinctive as a King Charles or a Tibetan, it often cannot be labelled.

The 'Black Spaniel'

In the mid-nineteenth century, and presumably earlier, there was a 'Black Spaniel'. Larger ones were described as black 'Springers', although they were not the only form of Springer around then, and smaller ones as merely 'Black Field Spaniels' or 'Black Spaniels'. Since spaniels had been divided into two classes, Springer (larger) and Cocker (smaller), the Black Spaniel probably included black versions of both.

26

In 1879 a noteworthy 'Black Spaniel' known as Kaffir was bred by a Thomas Jacobs in Newton Abbot, Devon. Kaffir was jet-black but was sired by a liver-coloured Sussex Spaniel called Bachelor. Mr Jacobs, however, believed that 'there never was a distinct breed' of 'Black Spaniel'; but nor did he believe, incidentally, that the Sussex was 'a distinct breed'. The dog Kaffir, who appeared to be more like a Cocker Spaniel than any other, won a first prize for the 'Best Spaniel' in a Birmingham show in 1880.

The Black was crossed frequently with the Sussex Spaniel to obtain shorter legs and a smoother coat. It was probably, indeed, just a mixture of other breeds crossed to produce a pure black dog with qualities from Springer, Cocker, Sussex and possibly Field Spaniels. Today it is the joint and several (as the lawyers say) responsibility of spaniel breeders not to go in for this exercise – not continually to 'breed in' to preserve a particular strain, since the result must in the end be physically and mentally deficient dogs, unsuitable for companions, pets or work.

The Irish Water Spaniel

While Cockers and Springers were making themselves useful in the coverts, another line of spaniels was emerging – the 'water spaniels'. Some dogs described as recently as the end of last century just do not exist today: they have either become extinct or have so altered that they are unrecognisable. But the 'water dog' has changed only its name.

Some early illustrations show a dog very much like today's Irish Water Spaniel, but that is not to say that there is no other ancestry in the bloodline. Various suggestions have been made – some mention the poodle and the curly-coated retriever (and some put it the other way round – that these dogs have water spaniel in their ancestry). Others include the Afghan hound, which is indeed an ancient breed that today shows a little of the cheery wilfulness of the Irish Water. The dogs that sailed with the Spanish Fleet in 1588 could well have been related to the Portuguese Water Dogs from the Algarve province, known locally as the *pelo encaracolado* (curly-coated one), and seen frequently with Spanish fishing fleets.

The Irish Water is a distinctive spaniel and one with a

personality all its own. It is the tallest of the spaniel breeds, with dogs about 53 to 58cm (21 to 23in) in height and bitches 51 to 55cm (20 to 22in). They weigh upwards of 27kg (60lb) and are the only spaniels with undocked tails – short and straight, tapering to a point at the end. They are eager, clowning dogs who love to show off. Often a 'one-owner' dog which can be somewhat suspicious of those it does not know well, the Irish Water Spaniel is loyal and intelligent, combining a good sense of companionship with working and guarding instincts. The face, throat, tail and fronts of the hocks are bare of the curly liver-coloured coat which covers the rest of the body.

The dog is a great lover of water, as its name suggests, and is a grand swimmer with a coat well suited to this. It has a good nose, is enthusiastic as a working dog and possesses great stamina with a strong, stocky body and a curious shambling gait which adds to its distinctiveness. It is especially suited to wildfowling. Its expression shows its cheerful character and rather wilful nature, accentuated by its curly top-knot and humorous eyes.

Much of the responsibility for the establishment of the breed is attributed to Justin McCarthy, whose dog Boatswain, born in 1834, lived to be eighteen. McCarthy expressed his view of the standard for the breed, which was much the same as it is today, in an article in *The Field*. He was much against crossing these dogs: they 'will not stand a cross with any other breed; the spaniel, setter, newfoundland dog and labrador dog . . . perfectly destroy coat, tail, ears and symmetry, added to which the cross-bred dog is very difficult to dry'. Some years later a Mr Skidmore of Nantwich, an authority on Irish Water Spaniels, extolled their virtues as tender retrievers and first-class working dogs for wildfowlers, at the same time describing them as 'companionable, full of fun and frolic'.

He spoke of three strains of the breed about at that time – one, known as the 'Tweed Irish Water Spaniel', was already almost extinct. He believed that the blood of the bloodhound could possibly be behind the breed, saying that having bred

Irish Water Spaniel Connie (Coinros Cherry Blossom) stands reflectively with her owner Miss Judy Hempstead

some – possibly the 'Tweed' strain – with dogs of the 'McCarthy type', they had pups with tan feet, cheeks and vents. The second variety, he said, was also almost extinct; it had short, sometimes crooked legs, a long body, close coat and featherless short ears. The third strain, he continued, was known as 'the McCarthy or south-country dog but without the coarse, truncated muzzle which McCarthy's dogs were alleged to have possessed'. Other writers of that time advocated large feet for the Irish Water Spaniel which spent much time in the water. This feature also marks a good specimen of the breed today.

Apparently around the time of McCarthy and Skidmore, there was also an English Water Spaniel, much used in duck-hunting in East Anglia. It died out shortly afterwards, which was put down to the rise of the retriever as a sporting dog, and the increased attention given to the Irish Water as a working dog, companion and all-round family dog.

The Irish Water Spaniels I have known have been extremely good companions with their warm, possessive, friendly and loyal natures and a gleam of mischief in their eyes. Those who know them well fall in love with them quickly; their characters are different from those of other spaniel breeds but there is much to recommend them.

The Brittany Spaniel

From France comes the Brittany Spaniel or Breton. This spaniel is French in origin, although its ancestry includes Irish and English blood too. Early in the last century, the Bretons had 12-inch-high spaniels with small, leaf-shaped ears and a featherless coat. They were fearless dogs, tackling all sorts of country in their working lives, first-class retrievers and good swimmers. These first Brittany Spaniels were crossed, some with English, others with Irish or Gordon, setters belonging to visiting gentry who brought them along when hunting quail and snipe in Brittany. The cross gave extra height. Brittany Spaniels are now up to about 51cm (20in) for a dog, and 46cm (18in) for a bitch.

Connie shows her clowning character, and the curly coat which makes the Irish Water Spaniel an ideal 'water dog'

Puk, a Brittany Spaniel, scents the air (Puk des Pigenettes, owned by Mr Stanley Smith)

The setter/Breton cross was especially successful, producing in the resulting offspring the useful characteristics of both breeds. The 'new' Brittany Spaniel is useful for hunting, pointing and retrieving, coursing the ground like a pointer and setter and retaining the speed and stamina of the earlier Breton. It works extremely well, for example, in woods – where the Breton people tie a small bell to its collar; when the bell stops tinkling the hunter knows the dog is on point.

Today's Brittany Spaniel is a highly versatile working dog. A registered UK breeder, Stanley Smith, who has done much to establish it here, will in fact only sell the puppies he breeds to people who undertake to work them. Also, however, it makes an extremely good companion, with expressive eyes and a gentle, trusting nature. It is the third most popular breed throughout the Continent, says Mr Smith, and the fifth most popular in the USA and Canada. In France the dog is popular both as a family pet and a working dog – an ideal dog for wildfowlers and country people, gamekeepers and family

Clumber Spaniel Toby (Mizzimoas Ambassador of Fraston) stands with owner Mrs F. Stanley

sportsmen who will work a good canine companion. It is fast and energetic, with a characteristic run, intelligent, obedient and friendly.

Ideal weights for the Brittany Spaniel are 15kg (33lb) for dogs and 13kg (28½lb) for bitches. It should ideally be shown as a compact dog with short, high-set ears, a flat coat with light wavy fringes, medium-length muzzle, short tail and darkish-coloured nose. Lack of pigment on the nose is a fault, as is a curly coat. Colour is normally orange-and-white, though there are some liver-and-whites, black-and-whites, roans and tricolours.

The Clumber Spaniel

This dignified but cheerful dog is the heaviest of British spaniels. It is often considered to be the odd-one-out, since it does not look much like the others: it is a massive breed, heavy-boned, long in the body and short in the leg.

The Clumber is a happy, thoughtful dog, faithful and with

a pleasing disposition. Its coat, an attractive white with lemon markings, sometimes with orange, is abundant, straight and silky. It is active, but walks with a characteristic 'rolling' gait, which is not perhaps surprising as some dogs reach 34kg (75lb) in weight. The usual weight is 25–32kg (55–70lb) for dogs and 20–27kg (45–60lb) for bitches.

There has been much controversy over the Clumber's ancestry. Though an 'odd' spaniel, it has many instantly recognisable spaniel traits. The 'first' appearance of the Clumber in England – or at least the one which has been most discussed since the end of the eighteenth century – was with the second Duke of Newcastle, who is said to have imported a group of these dogs from the kennels of the Duc de Noailles in France around 1770. There is little to support this theory: doubtless the Duke did have a team of Clumbers which was jealously guarded at Clumber Park in Nottinghamshire, but it is uncertain from where they came. It is even possible that other dogs of the same breed were around in England at about the same time: that the Clumber Park spaniels were the only ones seems unlikely, since the close interbreeding this would have involved would not have produced the hardy, healthy specimens of today. The Clumbers known to have belonged to such members of the aristocracy as the Duke of Portland, Lord Arthur Cecil and Earl Spencer in the late eighteenth century were probably descended from those at Clumber Park. Daniel's *Book of Rural Sports*, written early in the last century, supports the theory that the Clumber originally came from the Duc de Noailles, but then his classifications (and theories of dog origins) generally leave something to be desired in the light of what we know today. He simply classified all British dogs into three groups: 'The most generous kinds', 'farm dogs' and 'mongrels'. I have even heard a theory (in Spain, incidentally) that the Clumber was originally called the 'Columbus' dog, having come from Portugal, Spain or an Alpine region and been named, along with many other things, after Christopher Columbus.

Some have suggested that the dog is not a true spaniel at all, and others that 'earlier strains' were crossed with basset hounds. With the former I cannot agree, since the Clumber embodies many clues to the spaniel and its character resembles that of other members of the family. Of the association with the basset, it is true that often when a Clumber Spaniel sits up its coat rolls away (and is rather loosely folded), much like that of a basset hound in a similar position. My own feeling is that they are descended from the 'Alpine Spaniels' described by Cuvier in the late eighteenth century – about the time they were making a debut at Clumber Park. The Alpine was a distinctive lemon-and-white colour, like the Clumber. There are other similarities too – such as Cuvier's association between the Alpine and the Newfoundland and St Bernard: the Clumber has, in my opinion, an affinity with – and a marked similarity of appearance to – these breeds.

Some writers believe that the Clumber is in fact one of the oldest of spaniels and it could well have originated in Spain, being perhaps the 'white and tawny dog with a large head and body' mentioned by Edward of York in the fourteenth century. A breeder of Clumbers and Sussex in the nineteenth century, A. W. Langdale, also believed they had been around since the fourteenth century; he praised their talents for covert shooting in teams of nine. A fine specimen of the time was a Clumber called Lapis bred by Mr Arkwright of Sutton Scarsdale in 1875, and often illustrated. ·

Other, older, illustrations are often not so specific, and this is accentuated by the fact that Clumber bitches usually have more 'spaniel-like' heads than the dogs. Clumber owners often refer to a painting of 1788, by Wheatley, depicting the Duke of Newcastle and others accompanied by several Clumbers. The painting is called 'Return from Shooting' and the Clumbers shown are rather unlike Clumber dogs (they could of course be bitches) as we know them today – again perhaps a painter's interpretation rather than a difference in breed.

As working dogs they are slower than, for example, the Cocker or Springer. They are heavier, walking with a distinctly jaunty roll, and generally hunt mute. For this reason they were popular for covert shooting rather than for driving birds into the open. Indeed, those who bred and worked the Clumber in the nineteenth century often described them as being unsurpassed by any breed for this purpose. They were able to draw very close to game without disturbing it, and like the Breton owners of Brittany Spaniels, sportsmen working Clumbers sometimes fixed bells to the dogs' collars so that they could be located in the covert, and also so that the game could be gradually driven forward by the tinkling bells. It was then often referred to as a 'close and thorough' working dog – a description echoed by modern sportsmen. It was widely favoured too by Royal hunters in the late 1930s – which did much to popularise the working Clumber.

The Clumber is a noble breed, a good sound worker and a fine, amiable and intelligent companion – affectionate, adaptable and faithful, with a truly spaniel sense of cheerfulness combined with a remarkable air of well-earned dignity. It must of course have space and a careful training in puppyhood, if for no other reason than that it will grow up to be a large, heavy dog needing room to manoeuvre. Like all other members of the spaniel family, it also needs the sort of dialogue between dog and owner which gives scope for its intelligence and responsive nature, and for its need for involvement and praise.

The Sussex Spaniel

The Sussex Spaniel was of course first known in the English county of that name. It is another fairly heavy member of the spaniel family with a good nose and a similar (though less noticeable) rolling gait to the Clumber. It is a fine tracking dog, often becoming so enthusiastic when getting close to its quarry that it 'gives tongue': it has been said that the owner can often distinguish from the bark whether its quarry is furred or feathered! The Sussex is certainly a remarkable dog (being a man of Sussex myself, I like to think this has something to do with its place of origin) with sound intelligence and a good nature. It is a strong dog, remaining undaunted by the thickest vegetation when on a trail. It loves the country and rewards its owner with much enthusiasm on country walks. It is, unfortunately, rather rare today.

It has an abundant, flat coat, richly golden-liver in colour with a gold tip to the hair which emphasises its beauty. Height is about 38–40cm (15–16in) and dogs weigh about 20kg (45lb), bitches some 2kg (5lb) lighter.

Brown, a Sussex Spaniel, lifts her noble head as she is awakened from an armchair nap (Oldhobans Flashpoint, owned by Mrs Ann Findlay)

Though yet another old breed of dog, the Sussex is unlikely to be of as ancient a lineage as the Cocker and Springer in its present delightful form. It was definitely around in the county of Sussex during the eighteenth century, and was probably bred before that time, although early references are inconclusive.

It appears that the main breeding kennels for the Sussex Spaniel, a favourite with sportsmen at the time, were at Rosehill (near Heathfield) in Sussex. But the Rosehill Kennels were attacked by a disease, which writers around 1860 described as 'dumb madness': it might have been 'dumb' rabies or a less sinister affliction caused by inbreeding. About 1870, several Sussex gentlemen set about trying to rescue the breed from extinction and it is partly due to their stalwart efforts that we see this lovely and distinctive spaniel today.

There were several forms of Sussex Spaniel in 1870, and the Rosehill strain may have been the one which was 'rescued'; it is probably the forerunner of today's Sussex. Some of these Sussex forms were by no means pure Sussex and for a while the breed did not conform to the best of standards.

Two names appear regularly in the context of Sussex Spaniel discussions – Bowers and Langdale. The former is quoted as stating that the Sussex is 'beyond doubt' one of the oldest branches of the spaniel family although it was never a common dog. It was especially suited to hunting in dense woodland. The earlier Sussex Spaniels were trained to hunt feathered game only, and it has been suggested that their versatility in hunting fur as well as feather may be due to an early cross with a beagle – although in fact ancestors of almost every dog around have at some time been crossed with a member of another breed. It is impossible to say which strain our present-day spaniels come from. In 1867 a first prize was awarded at a Birmingham show to two liver-coloured spaniels with white markings and their breeder claimed that they were directly descended from the Sussex breed. Much controversy in the press resulted, and it was finally decided that a cross must have been introduced in order to produce liver-and-white specimens.

Other specimens were crossed with water spaniels and with the old black Cocker, but by 1875 the breed seems once again to have been sorted out and the main prizewinners at shows in the Sussex class appeared much more like those of today. At that time the best specimens were said to be found around Hawkhurst (now in Kent) and a standard gradually evolved. Youatt, writing well before this time, praised Sussex as a county for the finest spaniels (particularly Springers) and the fine breed known today was developed – and preserved in its purity of strain – in that county. It is perhaps no coincidence, too, that some of the best specimens are still bred in the county of Sussex, not far from Rosehill, at the home of Ann Findlay of Heathfield. Much is being done by a few to perpetuate an excellent companion and sporting dog.

The Sussex is thoroughly 'spaniel' in personality, being cheery, gentle, trusting, loyal and friendly. It has a very distinctive coat, walk and build.

Field Spaniel Winifred in appropriate surroundings (Bowgate Tanquist, owned by Mr Peter Riches)

The Field Spaniel

From the group of land spaniels which eventually became classified as Cockers and Springers emerged another with individual characteristics. This dog was lower to the ground than the other two breeds and longer in the body. It was developed primarily for sportsmen who preferred a heavier dog than the Cocker but with much the same personality. They wanted a dog which was active and full of stamina, with a docile, affectionate and gentle nature, soft in the mouth and a loyal companion.

The result, which we now know as the Field Spaniel, is a dog which makes a fine companion and efficient worker. It has a very attractive personality, great patience and an especially noble, graceful head with a long, slim muzzle. It usually has a flat or slightly wavy coat, silky in texture and in a variety of colours, but looks very well liver-coloured or mahogany-red. Other colours include black, roan and golden. Height is about 46cm (18in) and weight around 16–23kg (35–50lb).

The beautiful Field Spaniel is, regrettably, one of the rarer breeds around today, although efforts are being made to revive interest in the breed (and the Sussex). It has all the qualities of the spaniel family, which make it an excellent companion. One problem today, however, is that we are becoming short of country areas where these dogs are happiest and thrive to best advantage. It is perfectly possible to keep any member of the spaniel family in an urban area, but they all thrive best when they can have country walks and air rich with such interesting scents as rabbit, squirrel, woodland and field – rather than only the assaults of lead-filled petrol and acid rain.

The Tibetan Spaniel

This, though, is a dog equally at home in town or country. Many breeders may disagree with its inclusion in a book about spaniels; but after all it is called a spaniel and it *does* have many of the spaniel characteristics. It is a cheerful, intelligent little dog, unlike other spaniels in appearance but much like them in nature, temperament and personality. Sweet-tempered and docile, but proud in carriage and actions, it is also loyal and affectionate.

I know of one bitch with a Tibetan Spaniel sire and a Jack

The typical Tibetan Spaniel: a red-gold sable-coated bitch with a black mask (Kensing Rosetta, owned by Mrs Jane Lilley)

Russell terrier dam: she combines the inquisitive and tenacious qualities of the Russell with the sweeter nature of her sire, and is a delightful little dog. Many people would frown on this acquiesent attitude to hybridisation, but nonetheless all members of the litter from this cross had very attractive qualities.

The charming little Tibetan Spaniel has a silky double coat with a fluffy tail that curls back over its body, perky ears and a relatively short muzzle. It stands about 25.5cm (10in) high and weighs about 4–7kg (9–15lb). It can be seen in a variety of colours, champagne and fawn being two of the more popular.

Its ancestry is unknown, but these dogs are said to have been a favourite of the Dalai Lama and were certainly bred in the monasteries of Tibet – probably for many hundreds of years before they appeared in Western countries. Tibet's long isolation has not helped efforts to discover their origins. John White, writing in *The Kennel* of February 1911, said that he had owned 'Tibet Spaniels for many years', beginning with a black-and-white dog from the Royal Palace of Khatmandu. On its death that dog was replaced with an all-black one – apparently a common colour for early Tibetan Spaniels. This second dog, John White says, was obtained during the Sikhim Expedition of 1888. A picture of the Tibetan Spaniel accompanies the article and shows a dog somewhat different from today's: its general shape is similar, its tail curling across its back, but its muzzle is longer and its face less perky.

The same issue of *The Kennel* has a portrait of a black 'Tibet Spaniel' owned by the Hon Mrs McLaren Morrison of Northallerton; it is said to be one of some seven strains of the breed. This lady applauds their companionship, intelligence and affection. She apparently had not only black dogs but also 'golden', 'cream' and 'orange' specimens. She felt that the Tibetan Spaniel should not be 'shortfaced'. In 1911 Mrs Morrison was Hon Sec of a newly formed 'Tibet Spaniel, Lhasa Terrier and other Foreign Dog Club'. The Tibetan Spaniels of today are still not 'short-faced', though some people erroneously liken them to the Pekinese – and they do give you an interesting greeting which consists of snorting quickly into your face – inconvenient if you wear spectacles!

In their country of origin they were used as watchdogs, and their good eyesight and hearing, quick reactions and intelligence, remain notable today. In some circumstances a Tibetan could earn its keep as a watchdog – which could be one of the reasons for its survival in oriental courts. These little dogs may have been kept by travellers and traders using the trade routes between Tibet and China; there could after all be some link in the ancestries of Pekinese and Tibetan, although they are such different breeds today.

Much was done to establish the breed in Britain by Sir Edward and Lady Wakefield in the 1940s, and the Tibetan Spaniel Association was formed in 1958. Since then these delightful little animals, full of character and with a personality all their own, have grown considerably in popularity.

The Papillon or Butterfly Spaniel

The Papillon is somewhat similar to the Tibetan Spaniel (about the same height but shorter in the body). Again it looks very unlike spaniels in general, but in nature is a perky example of 'spanielism'. The French name *papillon* (butterfly) was given to this curious little dog because of its fringed ears, set obliquely on its head and looking like the wings of a butterfly.

The dog originated in France, although it was known in Spain and Italy, and the Spaniards kept it in Mexico, about the sixteenth century, when it was also known as the Dwarf Spaniel or the 'Squirrel Dog' – an allusion to the squirrel-like curve of the tail over the back. Its pricked ears and round, dark eyes add to the likeness. It has a long, thick, silky coat. After making the acquaintance of a Papillon you do notice some of the spaniel characteristics: it is cheery, alert, intelligent and friendly, and obviously wishes to participate in the activities of its home. These are not 'yappy' little dogs, and carry their daintiness in a dignified way, only barking when there is a need to do so. Being only 20 to 28cm (8 to 11in) high, they are particularly suitable for elderly people or others without the wish to take regular strenuous outside exercise. They cost less than the larger spaniels to feed, and make good companions for young and old alike. They are good family pets, though are not dogs for boisterous play.

The Papillon or Butterfly Spaniel shows off its 'butterfly' ears (Iffley Yvette, owned by Mrs Joyce Dunn)

The pretty little Papillon has also gained much popularity in the show-ring in recent years, producing some good lines.

A drop-eared variety of the Papillon is also around, though it is more difficult to find. Its ears still resemble the wings of a butterfly, but are dropped more in the spaniel way. This 'Drop-eared Papillon', known in various parts of Europe as the Continental Toy Spaniel, is always a parti-coloured dog, having a white coat with patches of virtually any of the other dog colours.

The King Charles Spaniel
While the Tibetan and the Papillon have become increasingly popular, sadly in recent years the King Charles has become less popular – and consequently less easily available. This is probably due in part to the wider availability of the Cavalier

The gentleness and dignity of the King Charles Spaniel is illustrated by D'Arcy and his daughter Mary as they take possession of a fireside chair (Huntglen Red D'Arcy and Huntglen Mary Stuart, owned by Mrs Madeline Harper)

King Charles. Many people are confused between these two, thinking them to be one and the same. They are of course quite different. Separate registration of the two breeds, distinguishing one from the other, was established in 1945.

The King Charles Spaniel is a compact, stocky dog with a deep wide chest, short straight legs and silky coat. It weighs only 3.5–6kg (8–14lb) and is about 25cm (10in) high. Its skull is large in comparison to the Cavalier's and, unlike the Cavalier, its head is domed. Its nose is shorter than the Cavalier's, and is turned up. It has a happy disposition, is loyal and affectionate. It is generally classed in four separate sections: the Blenheim (now a term used to describe the colouring of the dog – white with chestnut patches and a wide white blaze including the characteristic red forehead-spot), 'ruby' (rich chestnut-red), 'tri-colour' (white with black patches and tan markings) and the most usual 'black-and-tan' (rich glossy black with bright mahogany-tan markings).

The difficulty this breed often has in whelping – as other short-faced dogs do – is one reason for its unpopularity with commercial breeders. There is another reason though – apart from the 'competition' from the Cavalier King Charles – and this is rooted in its personality. It is a cheerful little dog but is perhaps over-loyal to those on whom it bestows its abundant affection: consequently it is highly sensitive and does not do well in kennels. So King Charles Spaniels need to be bred in small numbers in a home environment – where incidentally, they will do extremely well, despite sometimes having that problem with whelping. These are, as their earlier names of 'Spaniel Gentle' and 'Comforter' suggest, companion spaniels and they do put their hearts and souls into the job, showing undying loyalty to their owners, responding warmly to affection and desiring a lot of love and attention for themselves. They do not do well when left on their own or when away from the home fireside for long spells, and are not responsive to canine, rather than human, companionship. Madeline Harper of Ovingdean, one of the few breeders left who are dedicated to perpetuating King Charles in a home environment – she is also chairman of the King Charles Spaniel Association – points out that they take comfortable chairs and soft beds as their birthright. It is true – they need and enjoy their comforts and offer a high degree of companionship and affection in return.

About twenty-five years ago, some breeders of King Charles considered them too delicate even to run about outside and consequently the specimens around *were* delicate. Mrs Harper's dogs, by contrast, are brought up to be as independent as their characters will allow, and enjoy cavorting about on the Sussex Downs near their home. Though aristocratic by nature, they still have the fun-loving instincts of all the spaniel breeds.

Today, unfortunately, the handful of breeders of the King Charles have only a few puppies for sale each year, having to breed them in their homes because of the virtual impossibility of large-scale kennel breeding. Would-be owners therefore accept the nearest breed – the Cavalier (see below). But the scarcity of the King Charles remains regrettable, for it has its own distinctive personality. It has suffered through breeders'

45

and owners' over-protection on the one hand (poor, delicate specimens were bred years ago, reducing the numbers available), and through its own loyalties and faithfulness on the other.

Today, the few individuals in the hands of 'home' breeders are fine specimens and it is ironical that such a breed should be in danger of extinction. It has its own place in the spaniel hierarchy and there are many humans who would appreciate, and benefit from, the very special kind of companionship the King Charles offers. It is a grand, faithful little creature, with the qualities of 'spanielship' accentuated – perhaps almost to extinction. Let us hope that the breed will be preserved for those fine qualities.

The Cavalier King Charles Spaniel

The Cavalier is certainly less trouble to rear than the King Charles. It looks very different, with a much longer muzzle, a flat, instead of domed, head with high-set ears and a heavier, longer body.

Its coat is long and silky, without being curly, and it has quite noticeable feathering on ears, tail and legs. It weighs about 5.5 to 8kg (12 to 18lb) and the colours are as in the King Charles – usually Blenheim, black-and-tan, tri-colour or ruby.

The Cavalier King Charles, now so popular, has much to recommend it as a companion and a sporting animal. It is a winsome dog with what an old country breeder referred to as a 'happy tail'. More perky than aristocratic in its approach to life, it is extremely gentle in its ways.

Both the King Charles and the Cavalier are termed 'toy' dogs and King Charles II did in fact breed them; his brother, James II did much to popularise them. Neither king, however, initiated the breed, which was known some time before their reigns.

The Blenheim spaniel – that 'Comforter' and 'Spaniel Gentle' – the forefather of the King Charles and the Cavalier, is best known in the USA as the 'English Toy Spaniel'. The

Tri-coloured Cavalier King Charles Spaniel Heidi (Serontinas Christobel owned by G. R. & V. M. Coxwell)

early version of the King Charles and the Cavalier – the Blenheim-coloured Blenheim Spaniel – was probably much more like the Cavalier, with a longer muzzle at least; it was originally used for quietly flushing pheasants and partridges.

Former Spaniels

While the King Charles is becoming increasingly rare, some other spaniel breeds are now extinct. Some of these are depicted in old paintings. One, described as the 'Old English Spaniel', which was around in the seventeenth century, looked like a mixture of the Cocker (or Springer) and the Blenheim (King Charles) Spaniels. Perhaps that was one of the earliest Cavaliers. It was painted in more than one picture, for example by Van Dyck.

There was also the 'English Water Spaniel' mentioned earlier, which was almost extinct by the mid-1800s. Illustrations of the English Water Spaniel show it as something like a mixture of Irish Water and Cocker or Springer Spaniels. It may well have been the dog referred to by Dr Caius in Elizabethan times as 'Aquaticus', with long, rough, curled coat, used to retrieve wounded birds from the water. The blood of the English Water Spaniel may be in the veins of the Irish version – even if the ancestry is primarily from the Spanish and Portuguese Water Dogs. English Water Spaniels differed from today's Irish Water Spaniels in having no top-knot and a considerably shorter tail. They were very different dogs – both in appearance and in temperament.

There was also a somewhat mysterious 'Norfolk Spaniel' around – apparently similar in some ways to the Springer but with a thicker, coarser coat. It must have been crossed with many other breeds of spaniel; a connection with a Duke of Norfolk has been suggested but there is little foundation for the theory. The Norfolk was commonly liver-and-white, though earlier specimens were darker, some being black-and-white. In 1845 Youatt referred to the breed as being Springer crossed with a terrier, producing a 'black-and-tan variety'. It was, he stated, 'larger than the common Springer and stauncher and stouter'. It was reputedly a very loyal dog but more 'ill-tempered' (hardly the Springer blood – this would have made the dog the opposite of ill-tempered) and 'if not

48

well broken in is often exceedingly obstinate'.

The Norfolk may have been associated with the English Water Spaniel used for duck hunting in East Anglia. It was said to be a good retriever in the pursuit of fowl, taking readily to water, but was somewhat 'hard in mouth'. Many cross-bred spaniels at that time were dubbed 'Norfolks' and various sizes were around. This may well be why it became extinct as a recognised breed.

A 'Scottish Spaniel' too was once known, but is now extinct. This dog was apparently bred at Rossmore Castle in Scotland and was similar in appearance to an Irish setter, with a red-flecked white coat. It has not been seen since the early days of this century.

Other spaniels are still scattered around the world today – some being 'adaptations' of existing breeds – such as the American Cocker Spaniel, the American Water Spaniel (alias the Brown Water Spaniel), and the Northern Ireland Water Spaniel, which is a separate strain of Irish Water Spaniel. Throughout history various spaniels have been awarded all sorts of different names; some were only seen in paintings, others are the origins of current strains, altered on the way. So-called 'French Spaniels' for example, were the Picard (perhaps a strain of the Breton) and the Breton Spaniel itself. French Spaniels are rather like the Welsh Springer in style – long-coated, 55 to 60cm (22 to 24in) high (53 to 58cm [21 to 23in] for bitches). One of these in the past rejoiced in the alluring name of the 'Blue Spaniel of Picardy': it was blue or black roan, without the red-tan flecks of the Picard.

Another variation was the Pont Audemer Spaniel – a medium-sized dog, about 53 to 58cm (21 to 23in) high, with long curly ears, a docked tail and a long muzzle – giving the impression of a serious judge in a wig! Its legs were short and its chestnut-brown or mottled grey coat was wavy or slightly curly.

'Dutch Spaniels' are much like setters (the Drentsche Patrijhond). Though a small spaniel-like dog appeared in many old Flemish paintings, it may not have existed exactly as it was painted. Among the Dutch varieties is the 'Dutch Water Spaniel', similar again to the Irish Water Spaniel – a breed obviously destined to move around – with a black, brown or blue-roan, distinctly 'oily', coarse coat and a curly-haired head. It stands around 55cm (22in) high and is nick-named the 'Friesian Curly'. These dogs were used in otter-hunting years ago.

So there is much confusion about the ancestry of today's spaniels. There were probably several main lines, including chiefly the Irish Water Spaniel type and the land spaniel group of which Cockers and Springers were the most notable early members. Various breeds of spaniel in different parts of the world were probably being bred into different strains at the same time, and, as communications became easier, it became more possible to breed special qualities into a specific line. Those that became popular received much attention from breeders, who kept the strain going, and those less liked (or less useful for work) gradually died out or were 'improved' into other groups.

Spaniels in the USA

There is another group which, for the sake of simplicity, I will call the 'American Spaniels'. These include several spaniels which are really special versions or adaptations of those in the UK and Ireland. Some may have other European canine blood in their ancestry too, but they are all members of the spaniel family, and are bred to standards of the American Kennel Club. It will be seen in a later chapter that those standards differ from those of the English Kennel Club – largely of course, because the dogs themselves are different.

The American Kennel Club celebrated its centenary in 1983 – it was founded just ten years after the Kennel Club of Great Britain. Since that time it too has established its own collection of standards and done much to help improve the breeds.

American Spaniels include Field, Irish Water, Brittany, Clumber and Sussex. There is a Welsh Springer and an 'English Springer' (no American Springer), but this English Springer is very different from that bred in the UK. There is also an English Cocker (similar to the UK Cocker), an American Cocker (quite different) and an American Water Spaniel – which is rather like the Irish Water but without topknot and with a furry tail.

The American Water Spaniel (by courtesy of the American Kennel Club)

The American Water Spaniel appears to have the Irish Water Spaniel as an ancestor and, it is often suggested, the curly-coated retriever as well as the old English Water Spaniel, mentioned earlier and now extinct. This dog is mostly found in the Middle West of the USA and was, before the AKC recognition of the breed in 1940, used principally as a working gundog. It is a fine retrieving spaniel, often locating and retrieving several birds in one run, and an excellent swimmer. It has a loyal character, is eager like the Irish Water, and willing to please. It is usually solid liver or chocolate in colour, about 38–46cm (15–18in) high and weighs 13–19kg (28–42lb [dogs]) or 11–18kg (25–40lb [bitches]).

The Brittany Spaniel (or 'Brittany' as it is now called in the USA) is the only pointing spaniel recognised by the American Kennel Club at the time of writing. It is popular in the USA, first being introduced there in 1931 and becoming officially accepted three years later. In the first thirty years of competition in the USA, more than 150 Brittany Spaniels were titled 'Dual Champion' – a champion of both field and show. As in

Young Vicky shows that the American Cocker Spaniel is substantially different from the English breed (Lady Victoria of Serontinas, owned by Mrs Gillian King)

the UK, breeders of the Brittany Spaniel feel that it is happier as a working, hunting dog than merely as a companion, although it is indeed a companionable dog; like most friendly, willing dogs, it is relatively easy to train.

The Clumber Spaniel, though not widely accepted as a working dog in the United States, was registered there in 1883 and honours those who seek its company with its dignified presence. It is regarded as a fine retrieving dog.

Field trials for the American Cocker Spaniel were held in the USA by the Cocker Spaniel Field Trial Club in 1924, and the dog has evolved differently from the Cocker bred in England (and referred to in the US as the English Cocker). It has a much more feathered body, and distinctive markings on the cheeks and the sides of the muzzle, over each eye, under the tail and on feet and legs. The dog stands about 38cm (15in) high and the bitch 36cm (14in). The American Cocker has a definitive head with a pronounced stop (the indentation of the dog's forehead) and a rounded skull. In the United States it is popular both as a pet and a working dog, exhibiting the characteristic spaniel trustworthiness and adaptability. It is also becoming quite well known in the UK.

The English Cocker Spaniel (similar to the UK breed) is also bred in the USA, and in 1935 the English Cocker Spaniel Club of America was formed to promote the interests of the English Cocker and to discourage the interbreeding of English and American varieties. A pedigree search was made of the various English Cocker lines since 1892 and it was not until 1941 that the Club was ready to advise authoritatively on the problems of selection and breeding. In 1946 the American Kennel Club accepted the English Cocker Spaniel as a separate breed, and thereafter, at least, the breed has been applauded for its personality, including its faithfulness, alertness, courage, responsiveness, intelligence and merry disposition – the English Cocker in different parts of the world maintains its qualities.

The 'English Springer' of the USA (in Britain sometimes called the 'American Springer') is quite different from the English Springer Spaniel known and bred in the UK. An American Kennel Club standard was approved after the foundation of the English Springer Spaniel Trial Association in 1924 and was replaced in 1932 by another, thought to be better. The Association conducts field trials every year to show the merits of the spaniels as sporting dogs. They are generally considered to be working dogs rather than companions, and breeders are zealous in their efforts to prevent the breed becoming stocky or heavy-boned, which would, they maintain, reduce its usefulness in the field. It is still a willing, friendly dog, although the Welsh Springer (and the English version of the English Springer) are more typical spaniels in temperament, to my mind.

The Welsh Springer is also recognised in the USA and becoming quite popular there. It is, after all, a dog which like the Cocker has stood the test of centuries and its acceptance in the United States was long ago assured. It is also gaining

The American 'English Springer Spaniel' is really quite different from the breed in the UK (picture by courtesy of the American Kennel Club)

followers in India and Australia. American owners emphasise the need to train a 'Welshie' properly for hunting and also applaud its merits as a companion.

The Field Spaniel in America encountered some difficulties, as in England, due to the exaggerated features bred into earlier specimens in the nineteenth century and before – too much body length and heavy bones. Springer and Cocker crosses were introduced to eliminate these problems and when the Field Spaniel was introduced in America in the 1880s, in the shows it was only distinguished from Cockers by size. It is now a much improved breed, noticeably handsome, with straight forelegs and a height nearly equal to its length of body. It is recognised for its endurance, agility and intelligence. The official American standard for the Field is very similar to that of the English Kennel Club.

Four Irish Water Spaniels were first shown in the USA in 1877, one of which was imported from Ireland in 1873. The American standards for this breed are similar to those in England.

The Sussex Spaniel does not appear much in the United States; American sportsmen do not consider it to be fast enough. Because of its rarity, this fine spaniel's possibilities are not well known, but sporting conditions in America are substantially different from those in England.

This, then, represents the family of spaniels as it has emerged to the present day – as far as we know. Much interesting fact must have been lost. Spaniels have much in common among them, and in terms of affection, reliability, intelligence, loyalty and merry disposition, there are no better animals in my opinion. Those who work to preserve the breeds with responsibility, and with affection matching that of their charges, are to be applauded. Of course individuals vary; apart from the variety of personalities, it is true that some strains of spaniel, as of every dog breed, have flaws in their character, possibly as a result of in-breeding. This is why it is important to choose your particular spaniel carefully. You cannot meet its ancestors, but you can almost certainly meet its parents.

It is hoped that we can all play our part in ensuring that the good qualities evident in all breeds of spaniel never die out through neglect or lack of interest. Those who own spaniels should cherish them – for they are rare and remarkable companions with whom to share one's life.

3

Choosing a Spaniel

If you decide to have a spaniel – or even before – you need to look at some litters at breeding kennels. I say 'look at some' rather doubtfully, since I know how hard it is to resist buying one (or more) from the first litter you see of those delightful, cheeky little pups.

Before you actually buy a puppy, you need to think about the advice given in the next chapter, on 'puppies', and to decide on the sort of spaniel you will have. Where will you keep it? Do you have enough time to devote to its welfare? Where will you exercise it? Can you be sure you are going to make *it* happy or are you just buying it to make you (or your children) happy? Do you want a smaller type of spaniel or a large variety? Will you want it to work (sporting, shooting, etc), or will it be a pet only?

You have then to get the timing right. If you are working you need to select your time of purchasing. If possible, for example, arrange to take two weeks' holiday around the time of its second injection (aged twelve weeks) so that you can devote time to training it properly; and it will need a *lot* of your time when it first comes into your life, and for at least six months after.

If you are part of a family you all need to consider these questions. If you have small children the puppy will need even more of your time, and the association between puppy and child has to be worked out, for happiness on both sides.

To some extent your own habitat and way of life should affect your choice of spaniel. One of the reasons the Cocker became so popular following its success as 'Best in Show' at Crufts Show in 1930 and 1931, and then again in 1938, 1939 (the show was suspended during the Second World War years), 1948, 1949 and 1950, was that it was a suitable (and highly recommended) dog for all types of home and owner. The Cocker is adaptable enough to be happy in country or town, house or flat. It does, of course, need certain facilities –

rural walks, exercise, love and attention much of the time, interesting scents and a 'fun' environment, to name a few; but it is an adaptable dog with wide appeal – both in size and temperament.

By comparison, the Springer requires more rural activity, and the Welsh Springer in particular needs more outdoor life than a Cocker who has been brought up from a puppy in a town house.

It would be totally out of character for the Irish Water Spaniel to be happy in a city flat. It would be able to show you its best qualities in a country atmosphere with access to (and interest in) water. It is also a much more boisterous dog than, for example, the Cocker, and this should be considered when choosing or rejecting it.

The Clumber, though I have seen it kept very well in a small house, needs room to move about – and plenty of exercise. It is a relatively adaptable dog but its sheer weight and bulk make it best suited to a larger home.

The Field Spaniel is, of course, much happier (and more active) in a country home, but it is docile and gentle enough to do well with a companionable owner in a town environment provided that it is given regular country walks.

The Sussex is also a versatile dog. At its best running through acres of field, woodland or open country, getting itself thoroughly muddy, it will be equally happy curled up in an armchair in a town house when not outdoors with you.

The King Charles is at its best, on the other hand, seated or curled up comfortably in the best armchair in the house, by the fire, or on a bed. It loves – and demands – comfort and affection, and given these will be equally at home in a large or small house, flat or mansion. Although it does of course require outings, its real need is for the human company of its choice – that of its owner. (It is a matter for argument whether the King Charles owns its human or vice-versa!)

The Cavalier King Charles is more adaptable than the King Charles, but this means that it requires a little more activity – both exercise and space. There is, however, little difference in its needs as far as living accommodation is concerned, and the Cavalier is at home in town and country, house and flat.

The Tibetan and Papillon can be especially attractive

Toby in typical Clumber Spaniel pose (Mizzimoas Ambassador of Fraston, owned by Mrs F. Stanley)

Taking it easy on a favourite sofa is an aristocratic Tibetan Spaniel who has a wolf sable coat with pale gold fringes (Kensing Ra, owned by Mrs Jane Lilley)

companions to elderly people and to those with restricted accommodation. Being small, they need less food and exercise.

All members of the spaniel family have a common need: that of companionship – in terms of affection, regular exercise, an interest in the environment in which they live, and an outlet for their intelligence and sense of fun. Give them this and it will not matter if you keep a Clumber in a (large) flat – provided you exercise it a good deal; a Field in the town (provided you often take it into the country for a long walk) or a Springer in a suburban house. Establish its needs and fulfill these, and in general terms you will have a happy spaniel wherever you live.

If you live in the country and want a working dog who is also a fine companion, you have a choice between the Cocker, Springer (Welsh and English), Irish Water (for wildfowling especially), Field, Brittany, Sussex or Clumber – depending on the character and personalities most suited to your own way of life and personal preferences.

If you have a spaniel as a companion – no matter which breed – you need to be prepared to break off from what you are doing from time to time to fulfill the dog's needs – for play, exercise, feeding, or just companionship (in terms of close contact).

Once you have weighed up all the pros and cons and committed yourself to the short and long term responsibilities that spaniel-keeping brings, where do you go and what do you look for? It is always best to purchase a spaniel puppy from a reputable breeder. If you cannot easily find a good breeder of the spaniel of your choice in your area, you can contact the appropriate spaniel association or the Kennel Club. There is a list of useful addresses in Appendix 3 of this book which may help. This may seem hard on the appealing little faces in pet stores, but you do not know the backgrounds of these spaniels and some – especially those sold in markets – may be suspect. Market-stall selling of dogs (and indeed most pets) is a bad practice, for too often they are not well kept, and some suffer badly, not only from neglect but from disease.

If you know someone who has a lovable spaniel bitch

which has just had puppies, there is no reason why you should not buy one of these. Even then, it is as well to have some knowledge of the dog which sired the litter.

If you wish to become involved in the showing of spaniels, you need to look into a whole new set of ideas, to be explained later in this book. The breeder you approach for your dog will probably give you some tips on how to start, and indeed may well sell you a different pup from the one you would buy as a pet and companion, or as a potential working gundog. Prospective show dogs are more expensive than those wanted simply as companions, although the cost should not really be a factor in buying a puppy: whatever the price it will be a small one to pay for many years of very special companionship.

What About Buying an Adult Spaniel?

There are various guidelines which are useful when purchasing any breed of spaniel, whether or not the dog is for showing. But first, before discussing puppies, I should be fair and state that there is some merit in buying an adult dog if you find the thought of coping with a small puppy rather daunting. But be careful to discover an adult spaniel's background. The owner will give a glowing history of the dog, and may be telling you the truth; but that does not necessarily mean that the dog is right for *you*. A potential owner needs to spend some time with the dog to get to know it and to understand its quirks and preferences – as indeed it needs to know about you! Often there is a genuine reason for getting rid of the dog, such as the owners having a prolonged trip overseas; or they may say the dog just does not get on with children. Bearing in mind that it is always sad (and often suspicious) for anyone to get rid of an adult dog, you will have to judge the situation for yourself. You will probably know from your interview with the owners what sort of people they are and how the dog is treated. You will observe the dog's reaction to them – is it cowed with them? Is it over-boisterous?

I have had two dogs in this way – one a fine English Springer dog aged two, which had been trained, apparently found below standard for the gun, and sold to a couple who neglected him. He had a great personality and we became firm friends for about sixteen years. The second was a black Cocker bitch, five years old. She belonged to a publican with a family, and when they bought a boxer pup as a birthday present for their daughter the spaniel became jealous. This is a common problem which requires care. The family obviously mishandled the situation, for although the bitch snapped at them far too much, she could not have been gentler with my family. Never once was there any sign of a 'bad side' to her nature and she finally died at the age of twelve from a heart attack. She was an excellent dog. She came into a home where at that time there were no other dogs – a consideration to bear in mind. If you have dogs already, adding another adult dog is always a problem. Dogs have 'pecking orders', to some extent, if there are several in a home, and they work out some form of dominance and sub-mission tactics. To introduce another adult dog means that they all have to adjust. Sometimes it is difficult. If you already have a dog (or dogs), it is easier to introduce a puppy into the team: the puppy will grow to adjust, and the adults will not find him a threat.

My second wife had an Afghan hound when we married and I introduced a Cocker Spaniel bitch puppy to it. For some days the hound refused to eat while we were around, sulking and pretending to be very put out. Most Afghans (and this one was no exception) are difficult to control and their temperament and actions are usually unpredictable; but he soon settled very well with my spaniel bitch, recognising her as a good friend. Subsequently I bought another blue-roan Cocker Spaniel bitch puppy, and she too fitted in well; she has a good relationship with the other spaniel, but has tended to profess superiority to the Afghan; as it turned out, the youngest Cocker became the dominant member of the trio.

Dog or Bitch?
One question I am often asked is: do I prefer bitches to dogs? Personally I do, but that is my preference, and need not be yours. I have generally found bitches to be better companions, though even in my own experience there have been exceptions. Dogs tend to become sexy when a bitch in season is around the neighbourhood – I once had a dog which

would have made Houdini look a hopeless amateur when it came to escaping in pursuit of a lady friend. He climbed 6ft fences, wrenched chains and stakes from the ground, and even dragged a chicken house for some way before wedging it between two trees in order to detach himself from it. He was incorrigible, and although he was a great companion most of the time, he turned into a complex nuisance when he suspected there was a bitch in season around. But not all dogs are the same, and if you do have trouble with them in this way and have no intention of breeding from them, the vet can neuter them. It is a relatively simple operation these days.

Bitches do not behave in this way, despite the trend towards liberation of the female sex, but they do of course need watching when in season, about three weeks twice a year. If you take a bitch in season for walks where male dogs may be about, you need to keep her on a lead. Even then you should be prepared to ward off a selection of canine suitors. Picking up your spaniel will only exacerbate the situation – you may find having a large Wolfhound or Airedale wrapped around you a little unwelcome. However, if you keep a sharp lookout and rise early (before the local playboys of the dog world are up), a quick walk may be possible, even in urban areas. Various preparations are sold that help mask the scent of a bitch in season, but cunning males sometimes recognise these as what they are, and home in on them like a pin to a magnet. Spaniel bitches may also take great exception to having their tail-ends sprayed with a cold, evil-smelling preparation just before a walk – taking it as a substantial insult to their dignity. Veterinary Amplex tablets are an alternative but need to be administered four or five times daily during the season – a sometimes inconvenient task.

At the Breeders

Once you have decided to find a puppy and selected a breeder to visit (most breeders are only too pleased to show you their dogs, since this is the way they sell them), always telephone first to make an appointment rather than just 'dropping in'. If there are puppies available, the breeder will probably show you at least one of the parents, from which you can gauge the sort of dog your pup may grow into.

When seeing a puppy for the first time, watch for various points. Obviously, first of all the puppy must be healthy. Never buy an obviously physically defective puppy because it is cheaper. If you go to a good breeder you are unlikely to find any imperfect ones; but nonetheless, take care to choose the best one.

Watch the puppies on the move: straight limbs and a lively, confident movement without boisterousness mean a good puppy. Check that the one you like has good white teeth set right, and with the upper line of teeth resting over and on those in the lower jaw. Have a good look at the pups' underparts and at their coats. They should be free of any rashes and the coat should have a smooth, healthy look to it. The navel should be 'tidy' without any lumps which could indicate a possible hernia: this is not dangerous in itself, but it is better to have a puppy without it.

Spend some time with the puppies if there are several to choose from, making your choice the one which, after you have satisfied yourself about its soundness, still pleases you most.

It should have already been wormed by the breeder (and you need to do it again later). Ask the breeder for a diet sheet for the puppy for the following four months or so. Most breeders have these ready and will give you detailed advice on how to treat the puppy during the first few weeks you have it. They will also tell you about the pup's vaccination and, if the first one has already been given, will provide you with the vaccination certificates.

The breeder will provide a copy of its pedigree, and if you wish to do so will register the puppy's name at the Kennel Club. This *must* be done if you are to breed from it, so if you should decide on that later, write for a form if the breeder has not registered the puppy already (if he has you will need a transfer form), fill it in and return it to the Kennel Club with the appropriate fee.

Having settled all these details with the breeder (and paid!), you are now the proud owner of a spaniel. Take it home – in a box lined with a blanket and open at the top, if you are going by car – and take care of it.

4

Puppy Care

When you have the puppy home, you will soon discover that puppies are fun. The fact is, however, that they are demanding – they need a great deal of attention. The dog is forming its character and you will have much to do with that formation. You need to spend much time with it, to begin an association and friendship which will last for the dog's lifetime. Countless times I have been saddened to watch the vast enthusiasm shown by a human for a puppy gradually fade and sour, as the person comes to realise that a cuddly puppy sometimes does the wrong thing – and needs feeding regularly four times a day. Sometimes, much to my own chagrin, I hear of puppies being bought as Christmas presents for children who cannot look after them and indeed treat them as cuddly toys – until they become dogs, when they are 'disposed of'. Someone I knew professed to want a dog so much that she actually had three – each one remained for a few weeks before being given away as a 'nuisance' or a 'delinquent'. That lady, like too many other uninformed people, just did not realise what she was letting herself in for when buying a puppy. She would have been better off with a stuffed dog from the local toy shop! The association should not be entered into lightly. It is much like having one's own child, and the puppy needs nearly as much attention in its first few months.

Usually, once a puppy is chosen from the breeder, you must wait for a short while until it is able to leave the litter. Some breeders feel that the litter should stay together for a week or so after leaving the mother in order to establish a dog-learning pattern. In any event, before the puppy is to be collected, preparations are needed. These include, for example, getting ready a dog basket (remember the dog will grow) lined with a blanket; and in the early days a warm hot-water bottle well covered – particularly if the puppy is to arrive in the winter; also a spaniel feeding bowl, a dog brush, a first collar and lead (as the dog grows, a new collar and stronger lead may be wanted), and a water bowl. A few 'toys' which can belong to the puppy, and which it may chew to destruction, are important accessories: an old shoe or slipper is a good one, provided any metal pieces or eyelets are removed in case the puppy should swallow them. An old leather belt (with the buckle removed) can also be a good toy, and a couple of tennis balls, a rubber ring or other toys from the pet shop. Remember to introduce the toys to the puppy gradually and start it playing with them so that it is left in no doubt, as the weeks go by, that it can do what it likes with those things. Some puppies become quite attached to an object and carry it around with them throughout their puppyhood, while others play with a toy only now and then.

Spaniel bowl with convex sides to prevent long ears dipping inside

Before the puppy is collected, remember to get in a supply of the proper food. Diet and feeding times are of the utmost importance and should be strictly adhered to in the first six months. If a puppy lacks appetite for its food there is something wrong with it. It is natural for a puppy or adult dog to want to eat, and if it rejects its food for any length of time, even after you change the diet (sometimes this will help a 'fussy' dog), and if it has been wormed at the appropriate time, then seek veterinary advice.

Some puppies do have strange eating habits. They occasionally eat coal (if there is any around), and this should be discouraged, although in small doses it will do them no real harm. Others develop a habit of eating their own faeces or those of other dogs: this may be due to a lack of certain minerals in the puppy's diet, or it has been suggested that it is to do with the tendency some puppies have to eat the faeces

Sussex Spaniel puppies pictured here with Mrs Ann Findlay, a well-known breeder and judge who has done much to revive the Sussex breed

of their mother. It may be connected with introducing the right 'gut flora' (bacteria in the digestive tract) to a dog's system. It should in any case be discouraged and you will find that the puppy grows out of the habit quite quickly.

The breeder from whom you obtain your puppy will probably help if you are in doubt about its meals, and will in any case have told you what the puppy has been fed on so far. A typical diet sheet would be as follows:

8.30am:	Breakfast of milk and a cereal such as Weetabix, rusks, Farex or Shredded Wheat
12.30pm:	Meat mince and puppy biscuit, in equal amounts (50g [2oz] of meat and 50g [2oz] of biscuits)
4.30pm:	Scrambled egg with a little brown bread soaked in milk. Rice pudding is a possible alternative
8.30pm:	The midday meal repeated.

Note: Alternatives to mince can be tried gradually but should only be chicken, beef, lamb, white fish or a little tripe. Pork, liver or tinned dog food should not be fed at this stage.

The puppy needs food at all those times on time – in other words it needs feeding regularly every four hours throughout the day. This continues until it is three months old. During those first three months, new foods may be gradually introduced and the puppy's preferences determined.

At three months old you can reduce the meals to three a day. This is not easy to do all at once, and if you suddenly cut out a meal the puppy may well bother you. Eliminate one feed slowly, by bringing the 12.30pm and the 4.30pm feed closer together for about a week. Then give one of the two main meals towards mid-afternoon (a good time to feed your adult dog), omitting the late-morning feed first.

At four months the puppy can be fed just two meals a day, and this step can be introduced in a similar way, by gradually bringing the evening (8.30pm) feed closer to the main 4.30pm meal. Thereafter the puppy will be becoming more adult in its feeding habits, and you will probably start converting to the main feeding programme you have in mind. Puppy meal always needs to be soaked in water (use boiled water only). Make sure the food and water vessels are clean by running boiling water over them after washing. Drinking water, especially during the puppy's first few weeks, should also be boiled, but of course cooled before being put in the drinking-bowl. Clean water should be available to the dog at all times.

The amount of food given must gradually increase over the first six months but the exact amount depends largely on the dog. Watch that the puppy thrives but does not get fat. If it is fattening too quickly, it is being overfed. The first meals it gets (a total of 100g [4oz] at a time) will go up by a few more ounces as you reduce the number of times it is fed, but remember that an average adult Cocker Spaniel, for example, will probably only be eating about 200g (8oz) of meat plus about 150g (6oz) of biscuit on its main meal daily.

Your puppy will have been wormed by the breeder – probably twice – but should be wormed again at three months. Worming tablets can be purchased from a pet store or chemist. The dosage is given on the packet and depends on the weight of the dog. It is as well to worm all dogs regularly (about every 4–8 weeks). Modern worming tablets are quite palatable for spaniels and can easily be included in their dinner, or just given by hand.

Inoculations (against hard pad, viral hepatitis, leptospirosis and distemper) are of vital importance and it is stupid and irresponsible to let a puppy out on the streets, fields or parks before it has received both its inoculations from the veterinary surgeon: they are given, twice, between 8 and 12 weeks. Meanwhile the puppy can run in your own garden.

General care of puppies should be studied carefully and rules applied and maintained. The puppy will play with virtually any object it can get, and because its teeth worry it from time to time it will almost certainly chew things up. So give it something it may chew, and keep vulnerable objects out of reach. Children's toys are great fun to a puppy and such things as counters, marbles, pins, etc, any small and potentially dangerous objects, should be kept away. The natural puppy desire to play does bring potential dangers.

It is extremely good for a puppy to play and it should not be turned away when it wants you to join in. The act of playing can also be used to help in the learning process, matching commands to throwing a ball for retrieval, for example, or teaching the puppy not to jump up on you. Do not overdo the playing time or the tempo of the game: a puppy should not be rough-and-tumbled so much that it becomes over-excited. If you are playing a 'tug-of-war' type of game, remember that a puppy's teeth are not strong; let it, not you, pace the tugging. It will pull and tug and shake its head, and your part is to be 'anchor' at the other end. Never lift the dog up by its teeth – make sure it keeps its feet on the ground! I have found the best material for a tug-of-war is an old piece of denim – it is strong enough to be pulled, does not shed bits which get stuck in the puppy's throat, and does not tear easily. It will last for ages, but once it frays it should be discarded.

When playing with the puppy, and teaching it the commands which it will need as it grows up, be consistent – and see that the other members of your family understand what words of command will be used. If, for example, you will use the word 'fetch' to tell the dog to retrieve, use the word at the right time and stick to it. It will be useless if one person in the family uses the correct word and others choose their own; the puppy will become confused and then not respond at all. Training is covered in another chapter of this book, but with puppies there are two golden rules: always be consistent (in commands and in correcting the dog when it is wrong) and always be patient. Be firm but do not lose your temper. Soft but definite commands are needed, not shouting and shrieking – that approach leaves a nervous, confused dog. The spaniel loves to please and will do its best once it knows and understands what is required of it. It will be mischievous of course, from time to time, particularly in puppyhood, but you can leave it in no doubt of its misdemeanours without bellowing at it.

Consistency also has special significance in house training. Few dogs will purposely foul the house if shown at an early age not to do so. Give it a sharp tap on the behind with a rolled newspaper when showing it the mess, and then firmly put it outside – that will put the message across. If you are patient and faithfully take the puppy into the garden after it has eaten (and as soon as it wakes during the day), it will perform at those times, more often than not. On such occasions it should be warmly praised and its delight will become a house-trained habit. After a while (and when it gains some control over itself) it will begin to ask to go out when it feels the need. Remember that having learned to ask at the door to be let out, a puppy must be allowed to do so very quickly; it will not be its fault if it has an accident while waiting!

A puppy sleeps a good deal during the early months of its life – and it should be left to do so. Sleep is very important to a growing puppy (as it is to all dogs), and even though it appears angelic in a sleeping pose, it should not be disturbed until it wakes of its own accord. I have always found that a puppy that sometimes sleeps on a lap in its early life becomes very attached to the person it sleeps on. Of course there are many other factors involved in the formation of bonds of friendship, but sleeping on a warm lap without constant disturbance does help to build a sense of trust and security in its mind. My spaniel bitch Joanna often slept on my lap (I would sit still for an hour or so, reading and letting her lie sometimes in the strangest of positions); and it has contributed to the fact that nowadays she rarely leaves my side.

Puppies of all spaniel breeds do need training and respond very well to it. It provides them with security and interest and helps the bond between human and dog develop to its full extent. Some breeds, such as the Springer for example, become very much 'loners' if not given proper training and handling.

Get the puppy used to being handled at an early age. It is never too early to acquaint it with a brush, for example, or gently to examine its ears, mouth and feet. This will save much nervousness in later life. Most dogs enjoy a good brush, and being examined too, if it is done gently and firmly. Never underestimate the amount of care and attention a puppy needs in the first six months of its life. Every time it wakes it will want to relieve itself, explore, play or generally get into mischief. If other dogs are around it will often play

70

with them, but you should still be in contact with the puppy as much as possible during the day.

At night, though, a puppy can get used to being alone (or with the other dogs). A dog does not need to sleep on a human bed at night, nor need it be in the same room. It needs its own bed or basket in a warm, draught-free part of the house, with access to its water-bowl and a few of its toys, and then it should be content. If you start by feeling sorry for the appealing little animal and collect it from downstairs, bringing it into bed, it will soon catch on and cry, whine or even howl whenever it is left alone later. Its cries at night should generally be ignored; if it consistently cries, then of course it should be inspected briefly to see that it is not in pain, but having ascertained that it is all right physically, it should be firmly told to return to its bed, and be left. It will eventually (usually sooner than later) settle down. As the puppy grows it is a good idea to get it used to being alone in the house – for short spells only – as this will at least occasionally be necessary for the adult dog.

Also, get the dog used to travelling in a car. Most dogs travel quite well but some can be car-sick. Much of this can be avoided if the puppy is taken out for short journeys by car in its early life. If you have a passenger, then let a very young puppy sit on the passenger's lap (never have it on your own if you are driving – that is highly dangerous) until it gains an interest. Later it can be firmly relegated to the rear seat, or to the back if you have an estate car or hatchback. Car sickness which cannot be avoided or cured in this way by the time the dog has grown up may need medication from a veterinary surgeon. But it is rare enough for me to believe that it is usually temporary, of nervous origin, in puppies, and can be prevented by a little early familiarisation with the car and its movements. Also make sure that the dog gets a walk at the end of, or during, a journey; it then looks forward to a ride in the car. My own present family of dogs all enjoy it, after having become accustomed to it in puppyhood, they wait eagerly in the back of the estate car until they have had a walk and then settle down for the remainder of a journey. If we are visiting I always let them out when we arrive. Then they will settle peacefully in the car until I return.

Always remember that, if you *have* to leave a puppy (or an adult dog, for that matter) in a parked car, it must have a window part-opened, and must not be standing in the sun; also the dog must have a bowl of water there if it is to be left for more than a few minutes. Remember, too, that the direction of sunlight will change, and a car should therefore be parked in a place where it is entirely shaded. Heat worries spaniels noticeably and whether puppy or adult, they must have somewhere they can go that is cool – a shady spot in the house, car, garden, etc, when the weather is hot. No puppy or dog should be fed in the sunlight either, but indoors or in the shade outside.

So there is a great deal to do when a puppy joins the household. Above all it needs human contact and warmth, which you must provide regularly in large doses, along with the other requirements. Having a puppy about the house can be reckoned as a full-time job for at least three or four months. Thereafter you will reap what you have sown. The generally happy disposition of the spaniel will be liberally spiced with devotion to the one who has brought it up and who spends time with it and takes care of it.

Finally, a word about children. Most spaniels get on very well with children, small ones as well as larger ones, but no puppy, however playful it may be, is a children's toy. It should be treated with care, and just as you would not allow your own baby to be pulled about, teased or kicked around, so you should make sure that any young child is careful when playing with a puppy. Child and dog will soon grow to adore each other if the puppy receives kindness from its human playmate. This is also a training time for the child, a wonderful opportunity for him or her to learn to treat animals with the respect they deserve. He or she will grow to be a better adult as a result of the early tuition – and perhaps the next generation will be kinder to dogs, and other living things.

5

Breeding

If your puppy is a bitch, she may well have a litter at some time. You need (a) to have adequate space at home for her to have her pups and rear them in peace, (b) to prepare for it well in advance, and (c) to be satisfied that you can find good homes for the pups. Breeding from a bitch once in her lifetime may help to prevent breast tumours and other complications in later life, although it is by no means necessary. Before taking the decision to breed, it is best to have the bitch checked over by the veterinary surgeon, who will be able to tell you if there is any health reason why she should not be mated.

It should be mentioned, however, that by embarking on breeding, you increase the responsibilities you have – both to the canine community and to the spaniel breed. The sire and the dam should be carefully matched, making sure that there is no interbreeding. This can be assured by looking at the dog's pedigrees. Often in the past, bad breeding – interbreeding of related dogs to produce a particularly good 'showing' dog – has produced litters of defective dogs, frequently sold off as 'pets'. The dogs have had individual weaknesses in internal organs or had hysterical characters.

Anyone who breeds from a spaniel should firstly ensure that the resulting offspring will follow the typical spaniel character and preserve purity of breed, and secondly (and of equal importance) ensure that not one of the litter born will end up on the 'unwanted' dog list. There will probably be little difficulty in 'getting rid' of puppies: spaniel pups are particularly attractive and can be given away or sold with ease. That, however, is not the point. Unless you can be sure of finding all puppies good homes where they can remain throughout their lives – with owners who really care for them – don't breed. A poster I once saw effectively emphasised this point: it depicts a delightful little golden Cocker Spaniel pup and bears the words 'Before he dies he'll wish he was never born.' Do no let that apply to any puppies you breed! Make sure they all find *good* homes.

If you can cope with all this, you can in theory mate your bitch anytime after she has first come into season. But this can be too early. She is still very young, and I would not breed from a spaniel bitch under at least fifteen months old. Find a suitable stud dog – breeders will put you in touch with one, although it is not always sensible to go back to the breeder from whom you obtained your bitch, as the stud dog he or she recommends may well have serviced a relation to your own spaniel. Make a provisional booking with the owner of the chosen stud dog and confirm it when the season starts or your bitch 'shows colour'.

A bitch normally first comes into season at the age of about six months (although this is often delayed to nine or ten months). The season or 'heat' is in three stages: firstly a discharge of bright-coloured blood ('showing colour') for eight days or so – she will not, during this time, accept a dog. In the second phase, up to the fifteenth day, the vulva appears somewhat puffy, the colour of the blood discharge changes to a water-pink, and she will be ready to be mated. The last phase, from the fifteenth to the twenty-first day, is the time when her interest gradually wanes and the season comes to a close. The 'ripest' time for mating a bitch is on the tenth or thirteenth day, as a general rule.

Bitches vary considerably in their heat times and in the duration of them, and it is as well to observe them carefully throughout. As a rule of thumb, count twelve days from the day when the bitch is 'showing colour', and observe her closely as the day of mating comes nearer. False heats do occur sometimes – the bitch shows signs of coming into season but rapidly reverts to her usual self.

False pregnancies can also occur, whether or not a bitch has been mated. On these occasions she may have the appearance of carrying puppies and even produce milk. This is rather distressing for a bitch and she may require a sedative from the vet to calm her down. The condition appears to be the result of a hormone imbalance or change in the blood chemistry, and although it is not serious in itself, your spaniel will need much attention and reassurance while it is going on.

After mating has taken place (the bitch is usually taken to the stud dog and a fee paid for the 'service', although sometimes the stud-dog owner will claim 'pick of the litter' instead of a fee), both spaniel bitch and owner can sit back and wait for about five or six weeks. The gestation period (the time between conception and birth of the litter) is usually sixty-three days or nine weeks. Some whelp (give birth) a few days before and others a day or two later – as do most mammals, including humans. It is sensible to keep a 'whelping calendar' in a prominent position so that you can follow the progress of the pregnancy, take the necessary steps at the appropriate times, know what to look for and when to look for it, and be ready for the litter when it arrives.

There are also preparations to make beforehand. Make sure that the bitch's 'whelping box' – either her own basket, or a bed or a box made ready especially for her – is positioned in a quiet part of the house, in a warm, draught-free area. Some spaniels will have their puppies on your bed, under a table or in the best armchair – or any other place which takes their fancy – but you should try to be prepared anyway! About seven days are needed for a pregnant bitch to get used to unfamiliar surroundings if, for example, you wish to move her bed to a place which is more convenient for her to give birth.

Some people design fine 'whelping boxes' with removable lids, high sides (to prevent draughts), open fronts (to allow the bitch easy access and a ready escape from her demanding pups when she needs it), built-in heating pads and all sorts of other refinements. This is all very commendable, but can be wasted; the bitches I have owned have wandered around the contraptions, sniffing disdainfully. Sometimes, with a yawn of boredom, they have climbed in, settled themselves with a few grunts and groans, peered at me through doleful eyes (as only a spaniel can do) and pretended to go to sleep. Some of these bitches have persevered with their luxury cabins – but their pups have been produced, a week or so later, in widely assorted corners of the home. The fact that their own beds have been located in the 'best' positions has meant that they have happily retired to these, after having luxuriously given birth on, for example, the foot of my bed or under my desk.

Often it is possible to obtain a veterinary confirmation of pregnancy after about the fortieth day, but it is not always sure. There is no conclusive pregnancy test for dogs; most of it is a wait-and-see routine.

Around the fortieth day, an improvement in the quality of the spaniel's food should commence. She requires extra milk and vitamins, including A and D, along with her favourite menus. Do not overdo it: increase her food intake gradually with the emphasis on quality rather than quantity. When she is near to whelping she will probably eat less. Do not tire her with too much exercise just before she is ready, and let her make her own pace, both in eating and exercise. If you are worried, then telephone the veterinary surgeon for advice. You will also feel much surer in your own mind if you have her checked over by the vet around the fortieth day, and he may well at that time make an appointment for a further check-up nearer her time of whelping.

Just before the time when your spaniel bitch is to give birth, her temperature drops to below 38°C (100°F). Labour pains follow shortly afterwards. Slight straining will be evident, especially across the back (that is if you are in time to see it), and this is increased to about three or four straining sessions in about three minutes. The water bag makes its appearance, about the size of a squash ball, and breaks to release the cushion of water.

The bitch licks around herself, and shortly after this the first puppy appears. It usually arrives head-first, but a 'breech' birth, when the feet come through first, is not uncommon and should not normally give any trouble. If the bitch has still not given birth to the first puppy in about one-and-a-half hours from starting labour, the veterinary surgeon should be contacted as there may be some reason for the delay. If a Caesarian section is necessary, it should be carried out during these early stages of labour, and although it may cost the lives of some of the puppies, it does not usually cause damage to the bitch herself, though it is not a pleasant experience for her. It is not often needed; the majority of births progress quite smoothly, with each puppy making its debut in a membrane or bag which is then broken by the mother. If she delays, you should help release the puppy, as it cannot inflate its lungs with air until it is out of this sac. It may also need its mouth and nose cleaned up a little, but usually the mother is capable of this sort of attention, massaging the little body gently to spark off the initial intake of breath.

The puppy will be born blind and connected via its umbilical cord to the placenta (afterbirth), which should be expelled by the mother after the puppy. If it is slow in following it can be gently pulled out via the cord attached to the puppy, making sure there is no strain at the end attached to the puppy, as this will cause a hernia. A piece of umbilical tape or other sterilised thread can be tied about an inch from the puppy's navel and cut with a sterilised pair of scissors on the opposite side of the thread from the puppy. Normally all this is unnecessary, because the mother will have bitten through the cord herself, but on occasions, a bitch – especially a youngster – neglects this step and it must then be done for her.

Each puppy is accompanied by its own placenta and usually the bitch eats these herself. Do not prevent her from doing so – it will probably do her good since dogs (and most other mammals) have from the beginning of time consumed their placentas. However, it is important to keep an eye on this, just to ensure that no placentas are left behind in the mother; check that there is one placenta per puppy. If any are missing, then contact the vet, since if a placenta is retained it could lead to uterine sepsis later on.

The bitch will not give birth to all her puppies in one rush, and may take a short nap in between births. Keep an eye on her and if she gets into difficulties (straining, becoming weaker, etc), then get in touch with the vet. She will spend much effort in cleaning up herself and her pups when the delivery is complete. She should then be encouraged to have a drink of milk and water mixed with a teaspoonful of glucose or honey, and may want to go into the garden to relieve herself. Take that opportunity to clean up or replace any bedding and inspect the pups for any obvious problems.

After this the mother needs rest and quiet – not an endless procession of people coming and going to admire her offspring. No strangers should come close to her for at least two days and any other animals in the house should be kept away. The birth is tiring, and for at least twenty-four hours the mother needs a liquid diet, consisting of milk, water, honey and/or glucose, about five times within that period. On the second day, if her temperature is back to normal and there are no complications, she still needs a liquid diet, but this can be alternated with light solids such as scrambled egg, boiled fish (make sure there are no bones in it) if she enjoys fish, and a little raw or lightly cooked minced beef. She will need more if the litter is large (about five or six). Fresh raw meat and a good supply of clean cold water will help her milk supply and assist her in gaining strength. Eggs are always a good supplement, but too much milk in the diet may cause diarrhoea.

If you are helping a bitch in her whelping, try not to show anxiety; this can be transmitted to her and may escalate her own anxiety after the birth. One of my sons actually assisted his bitch right through her birth, helping her four puppies into the world with a calm which is characteristic of him. He just happened to be there and did what he thought was best for her. She was delighted with her pups, showing no anxiety whatsoever after they had been born and thoroughly enjoyed showing them off. I am sure much of it was due to the unworried help she had from my son – who was eight years old at the time.

The pups' tails should be docked on about the third day, if they were born on time, on the fourth day if they were premature. (This of course is not done with the long-tailed varieties such as the Irish Water Spaniel.) The veterinary surgeon will do this quickly and simply, and will remove the dew claws (the dog's fifth digit in rudimentary form, on the inside of each foreleg). These are a continual nuisance to a dog if left on, catching in bushes and grasses and becoming torn and often ingrowing. The vet can also take the opportunity to check over the puppies and their mother.

If a bitch has a small litter, she may have excess milk. This can be a painful condition for her and will need relieving. The milk glands appear lumpy and are hard to touch. Stand up the spaniel on her hind legs and use thumb and forefinger to press the milk through the teats so that the lumpiness is gradually lessened. Give her less liquid. If the litter is still alive the condition will probably last only whilst the puppies are very young, since as they grow older their intake and the flow of milk will adjust accordingly. If the litter has been lost, then the vet should curtail the production of milk with medication.

There are occasions when the spaniel breeder will be called upon to rear a litter by hand – in the event of a particularly large litter, for example, or if the dam has mastitis. This is extremely demanding but nonetheless rewarding. No achievement can compare with that of being entirely responsible for ensuring that a young creature continues to live through one's own efforts. Hand-reared puppies need small amounts of food every two hours – day and night – for at least a week. After the first week, you feed every three hours through the night and at two-hour intervals during the day. It is an extremely tiring task but one which allows you to observe at first hand the miraculous growth and development of the young spaniel.

Milk is a subject of prime importance to the survival of orphaned puppies and those that need feeding by hand. The milk of your spaniel bitch is better food than cow's milk, for example, being richer in protein (about 7.5 per cent compared with 3.4 per cent in cow's) and in fat (about 11 per cent compared with about 3.8 per cent in cow's); if you are using cow's milk as a substitute, these differences need taking into account. Goat's milk is closer to dog's milk, having around 4 per cent protein content and about 6 per cent fat, but it may be more difficult to obtain. Adding an egg yolk and two drops of pure cod-liver oil to a pint of cow's or goat's milk will roughly compensate for the difference.

Temperature is also important for newborn pups; if they should chill they will die. The room temperature in which they are reared should be kept at between 24 and 29°C (75 and 85°F) for at least the first six days of life. It can then be gradually reduced to between 21 and 24°C (70 and 75°F) for the next three weeks or so. They should also be kept well out of draughts and away from noise and general disturbances.

It is also vital that all contact with the puppies should be very clean. If the mother has been lost, or has not been with the puppies during the first two or three days of their lives, they will have lost the transmission of protective antibodies that is given them through their mother's licking. The possibility of infection will be that much greater.

The easiest way (if there is one) of feeding tiny puppies in the first few days of their life is by means of a small-diameter flexible rubber tube attached to a syringe. (The size of the syringe nozzle will determine the diameter of the tube.) A measured amount of goat's-milk mixture (as described above) or baby-formula milk is drawn into the syringe and the end of the rubber tube gently and gradually eased into the puppy's throat. As the tube goes down the puppy will swallow it – it is necessary that it does, to ensure that liquid is not pushed down into the lungs. When the tube is well down into the oesophagus (this can be judged by the length of the neck of the puppy), the warm liquid is very gently pushed through the tube by depressing the plunger of the syringe.

About 1–2ml should be given for a puppy weighing between 300 and 700g (10 and 25oz) and the feeding process will take about two minutes, after which the tube should be gently withdrawn. Some puppies will suck from a teat on a bottle, but they need to be very relaxed to cope successfully with this method and it usually takes longer than two minutes! After two or three days the quantity may be gradually increased, until it is doubled as they grow. If in doubt seek the advice of your vet – especially if the puppies are not evidently thriving well. One other important point – ensure that the pup urinates and defaecates after each feeding. If it does not readily do so, then gently massage the abdomen with some warm cotton wool or lint to encourage it. The dam will carry out this task when nursing her pups by softly licking them – thereby preventing them from becoming constipated, which would endanger their lives.

Puppies open their eyes at about two weeks old and the next – and probably one of the most important – milestones in their life will be weaning. It should be started at around three to four weeks old, though this rather depends on the milk supply of the mother. A good milk substitute, which can be obtained from the chemist, will be the first step. It is supplied in powder form – such as Lactol – and a heaped tea-

A quartet of Welsh Springer Spaniel puppies put in an appearance at their kennel doorway: four individual characters from the same litter, as can be seen from their different expressions (owned by Mr & Mrs J. S. Walton)

spoonful should be added to boiled hot water and mixed to a thick paste; then more hot water is added. About five tea-spoonfuls will be enough on a clean saucer (pour boiling water over it). When it has cooled to no more than body temperature the puppy is encouraged to poke its nose into it. As with a baby, after blowing a good deal of it over you, it will soon catch on to the idea and lap it up. This feed should be given once a day for three days (the mother will still be feeding the puppies herself at this stage), and twice a day three days later. At this stage a little cow's milk can be added to the mixture, gradually substituting it for the water content.

After the puppies have been splashing around in their new feed for about three days, small amounts of minced beef can be added. Later, when they are used to it, provide them with the four meals a day which will start the routine of their feeding habits for at least six weeks. A milk-base meal at 8.30am is followed by a meat-based feed at 12.30pm, another milk meal at 4.30pm, and finally a meat meal at 8.30pm. The milk from the mother will by this time have dried up and the puppies will become dependent on the human feeding routine.

The mother's diet should not be neglected either; she will need building up. Her intake of fluids can be reduced and her system reinforced with fresh meat, raw and scrambled eggs, some biscuit meal and cereals. Sometimes a mother will regurgitate some of her food for the puppies, and although this is a messy process, there is no cause for alarm. Wild dogs regularly do this to help wean their young. However, if the mother is regurgitating some of her own food for a few days, her diet should be supplemented to compensate.

When a puppy is around six weeks old (and getting ready for the outside world and all its hazards), a full diet sheet can be worked out for it, gradually bringing in regular meals with more variety. A typical diet sheet at this stage is given in Chapter 4, Puppy Care.

Removal of puppies to their new homes (or from the mother) should be arranged at intervals so that the mother does not feel the immediate loss. You will probably find at least one of the puppies (preferably a bitch) so irresistible that you cannot part with it – and that is often how a family of spaniels is built up!

If you have more than one spaniel, they all need the same affection and attention to their welfare, the same consideration and the same companionship. Spaniels are great individualists – and each one therefore will have its own personality – but they will have the same needs. Often an owner will come closer to one dog than the others and this cannot be avoided when affection is involved, but do not show favouritism; this promotes jealousy and will wreck the best of happy families. There is no reason why one dog should not receive special attention sometimes, but when another spaniel comes into the game, or just joins the 'discussion', do not exclude it. Spaniels can be hurt easily, and if offended, need some special attention in compensation. Be aware of this part of their nature and you will have a happy 'family' if you do decide to keep more than one of these remarkable dogs.

6

Feeding

Feeding spaniels depends largely on three factors – what the dog likes, what is good for it, and what it should ideally weigh. A fat, or even portly, dog tends towards being an unhealthy dog. As in humans a slim, trim figure is best for good health.

A balanced diet is most important. This, in general terms, means meat and biscuit backed up with occasional vitamins and such 'tasty' foods as eggs, fish, etc. Many farm dogs – in fine condition – exist on 'scrap feeding' with bread and milk as a regular diet – so there is no golden rule for just what a dog should be fed; but there certainly *are* good guidelines. Most dogs enjoy a variety, and meals supplemented with the right sorts of household scraps often provide that variety.

My own dogs do very well, keep in good trim and generally in good health, on a high-grade tinned dog food and a good biscuit meal soaked in either hot water or beef (or similar) gravy. At least once or twice a week they receive some extra vitamins in powder form sprinkled on their food, a teaspoonful either of olive oil (summer) or cod-liver oil (winter), and a raw egg each. Occasionally the tinned food is replaced with lightly cooked ox-cheek or chicken, and a little plain boiled rice instead of the biscuit meal.

They are fed a main meal once a day, in late afternoon, and have a breakfast of a half a scrambled egg each and brown bread soaked in a little milk. They have a dog biscuit or two during the day and a gnaw now and again at a large beef thigh-bone in its raw state. If they put on a little weight, the proportion of biscuit to meat is reduced and exercise slightly increased until they are trim again. They are never fed by the family at the table, but get suitable household left-over scraps like meat trimmings, vegetables, etc (if not highly spiced or too stodgy), in their dinner. They enjoy a titbit of apple, cheese or carrot too.

But you might buy a spaniel, follow my diet strictly (once

he or she is adult), and find that the dog just does not enjoy it. Dogs, like humans, have preferences. It is the preferences that need to be kept within bounds. They *should* have meat and they *should* have a good supplemented biscuit meal, but they may prefer a particular type of meat, such as raw tripe, horsemeat, an individual variety of tinned dog food, and so on. What is important is to ensure that they are not encouraged in preferences which do them harm – like boiled sweets, for example, or potato salad or jam roly-poly. Many dogs will eat anything, within reason and sometimes without reason, and just because your family likes a food, it does not follow that it is good for the dog! So the golden rule is – find out what the dog enjoys most but keep the diet as simple as possible within the best nutritional requirements.

An incorrect diet may put weight on, and will almost certainly upset the dog's stomach, causing diarrhoea and discomfort. It will also be reflected in a dull coat, lack of energy, dull eyes and sometimes a dry nose and irritability. You may say that the way I feed my dogs is expensive; yes, but good-quality feeding for your spaniel (as indeed for humans) is worthwhile in the long run. Best feeding does *not* mean giving the dog the best human food.

In specific terms a spaniel needs protein, fats and carbohydrates in the right proportions. Protein can be found in meat, fish, eggs and cheese, for example, while cereal, bread (brown) and dog biscuit (not sweet 'human' biscuits) will supply carbohydrate. Fats are found in milk (though too much will probably make the dog 'loose'), fish oils and the fat regularly found on meat. One main meal, preferably in the late afternoon or evening, suits most dogs, with a 'morning snack' of either a few dog biscuits or such light additions as scrambled egg, a little fish in milk, etc.

Cut the dog's food into easy-to-manage pieces, since even a single dog, not competing with another, will usually bolt its food. A dog does not use its teeth as we do, and having stronger digestive juices in the stomach, will break up its food after swallowing. The dishes should be big enough and clean. There is a special 'spaniel bowl' shaped with a curved top so that the dog's long ears fall outside it when eating. This keeps the ears clean and saves messy tangles.

Some raw meat is good for the dog (although some dogs will not touch it), but in any case if you are cooking dog meat, such as ox-cheek, liver, horsemeat, etc, only do so lightly. Also ensure that the food is not scalding hot when put in the dog's dish. Dog biscuit should be soaked either in an Oxo-type gravy or hot water, and should only be warm when served. Tinned dog meat is a good alternative to fresh meat. Your dog will probably choose his own if you let him try several different varieties, but generally the firmer type is more acceptable. (Pedigree Chum is at present the one chosen by my own dogs, though they also like Pal.) Biscuit, too, varies somewhat, but a good one, like most good tinned dog meat, contains vitamins and minerals necessary for the dog's general health. The addition of an egg once or twice a week, and/or some fish or cheese (not too much), helps the dog. Left-over vegetables such as greens, carrots, etc, can also be included. The raw egg helps the coat of a spaniel to shine and exhibit its good health.

As far as bones are concerned, some people say that 'nothing has ever happened to my dogs and they eat and enjoy many different bones'. But my advice is *not* to feed spaniels all sorts of bones. Accidents *do* often occur – small bones get caught in a dog's throat, wedged along the jaw, stuck in the cheek or even swallowed to cause internal damage by sharp points. Give large marrow or knuckle bones, which stimulate gastric juices and which spaniels enjoy. The marrow adds extra vitamins and calcium and the whole exercise helps to clean the dog's teeth. One of my spaniels regularly brought her marrow bones to me after she had gnawed them for an hour or so, and dropped them at my feet, knowing that I would extract the marrow for her with a meat skewer. The marrow is especially good for dogs and this added titbit is always enjoyed. The habit has been continued with all my dogs, so I eventually take their bones away for this purpose; after extracting the marrow, I remove any left-over small pieces of bone and dispose of them unnoticed!

Water – fresh and clean – must always be available to the spaniel. Dogs vary in their drinking frequencies of course, but they do get their water dirty very quickly and a clean supply, maybe changed several times a day, is essential. The

85

occasional addition of a block of sulphur obtained from your local pet store especially to put in their water bowl does some good as a 'blood purifier'.

Feeding programmes need to be studied in conjunction with the dog's appetite and preferences. If you start with a new puppy, as it is gradually changed over from puppy food to adult dog food you get to know its likes and dislikes. The secret of successful feeding, as of every other form of association with the spaniel, is to study the dog and its reactions. As you get to know your dog, you become acquainted with its 'language' – signs and signals which indicate its preferences, its state of health, its comfort. Much can also be learned by watching the dog defaecate. If it has diarrhoea regularly, then something is wrong – probably with its food.

I once met an old lady who had a very fat Cocker Spaniel. She came to see me because she had heard that I kept spaniels, and thought I might know why her dog was getting fat. She had not been to the vet because there was really nothing wrong with her dog – except that she was fat. When I first saw the dog I realised that the term 'fat' was an extreme understatement. The dog was grossly overweight and waddled along (still cheerily wagging her rear end, rather like an air balloon in a high wind), puffing and huffing like a steam engine. I was alarmed by the sight of the poor dog and tried to impart this emotion to her well-meaning owner, telling her that the dog *must* go on a slimming diet right away or it would probably die of heart failure. The old lady was flabbergasted, she said, because her dog seemed so fit in every other way. She went on to tell me that her dog did not eat much, as it was – she just got fat! It turned out, however, that she was feeding the dog exactly what she ate herself every day. As her own diet consisted of cereal, egg and bacon for breakfast, coffee and biscuits at eleven, a 'light lunch', tea and biscuits at four and dinner at seven, the poor dog spent most of its life eating. 'Even then', she said, 'she doesn't eat all of it – she doesn't like fruit pies, except for some of the pastry, and she won't look at runner beans!' She did, I learnt later, also join her mistress in a six o'clock glass of sherry.

This well-meaning old lady would have killed her beloved dog through her efforts to be kind, in a matter of months. I wrote out a diet sheet and promised to call and see the dog in a week. The two waddled off, the dog puffing and her owner with tears in her eyes. She did keep the dog to the diet, however, which consisted mainly of fish, raw meat, chicken, eggs and small amounts of cereals (the variety had to be maintained to keep the dog's interest); and the dog duly began to lose weight until it was relatively trim. As its energy increased and it enjoyed its exercise much more in the years to follow, it also improved its owner's life and shape, and I often had the odd chuckle as I saw them both trotting down to the park twice a day – the lady puffing just a little and the dog in fine trim.

Incidentally, I found a diet sheet recently from a spaniel breeder of the mid-nineteenth century, which included much in the way of 'raw flesh'. It is, said the breeder, 'their natural food'. Apart from advocating the supply of goat's milk to puppies – still a good tip today – he gave his dogs 'oatmeal boiled with sheeps' heads and butchers' scraps' twice a day, the second meal being reinforced with raw meat in limited quantities. 'Do not overfeed', stressed the breeder, 'or you will make a pretty mess of them.' Sound advice indeed.

Some dogs eat slowly, others eat fast; if there is more than one dog eating at once this speeds up the mealtime noticeably, though each should have a separate dish, placed within sight of each other but definitely apart, otherwise the faster eaters tend to polish off the food intended for the others. At the end of a good meal you may hear your spaniel belch – a sign generally that sufficient food has been eaten.

The quantity of food needed varies of course according to the spaniel. A Cocker Spaniel should be fed about 200g (½lb) of meat daily with biscuit meal regulated to suit its weight (about a small handful before soaking – around 150g [6oz] – is usually enough). A larger breed, such as a Springer, would probably find upwards of about 700g (1½lb) of meat more in line with its needs. Dogs should, wherever possible, be fed at the same time, or times, each day. They are happy in a mealtime routine and variation only upsets them. Meals are very exciting events and the spaniel should be encouraged to enjoy them!

7

Handling and Grooming

'Handling' is an aspect of training, so is discussed in the next chapter. However, handling itself is really 'care' and begins as soon as the puppy is purchased. Gentle handling in puppy-hood reaps rewards in later life and one cannot begin to handle a puppy too soon once it has left the breeder. 'Gentling' is a term often used in the world of horses but it is a good description of the contact process a puppy has with the best owners, as it grows into a dog and throughout its life. Gentling, in my vocabulary, means keeping the spaniel at ease by various means in times of stress and is an integral part of contact between dog and owner.

Spaniels, right from early puppyhood, enjoy having their ears gently fondled and chests rubbed. Bitches, I have found, usually much appreciate having the abdomen gently rubbed. Always stroke a dog the way its hair runs – that is from head to tail and not up from tail to head. As you get the spaniel puppy used to being handled from the beginning of its life, you can regularly examine its mouth, eyes, ears, feet, tail and teeth. A puppy which is gently fondled early in life usually loses any initial nervousness. The gentle handling of a dog helps it to *trust*, and that is the most important ingredient of a relationship. You must earn the dog's trust and respect – the former by firm but gentle handling, soft words, affection and guidance; the latter usually by training, leadership and encouragement; both trust and respect are earned in the general mix of the spaniel's life.

Soft words are an essential part of a spaniel-human relationship. Loud noises are amplified many times by a spaniel's delicate hearing and shouting only bewilders it, adding to any existing nervousness.

When making a spaniel's acquaintance for the first time, go down to its level and extend a hand towards it. The dog – eager or nervous – will approach. Let it get to know you by taking its own time to inspect. If it is nervous or suspicious it will take longer and you may have to ignore it after the initial introduction. It will then inspect you from a distance, and if it wishes the distance will gradually be reduced until it is sniffing around you. When this has been going on for a minute or two, you may again gently extend a hand towards the dog, letting it sniff it slowly. Some dogs do not like being stroked by strangers and it is something the stranger must accept. After all, it has taken much time for the owner to win the dog's full confidence, so why should a stranger expect more?

You will enjoy watching your spaniel develop its own characteristics, its own personality, developed from its heredity and the influences of its environment and upbringing. My two spaniel bitches for example behave very differently from each other in all sorts of circumstances. Squirrel-chasing is just one example. I often take them to a wood where there are many squirrels and they delight in sniffing out the little creatures and chasing them up a tree. Sometimes the chosen squirrel gives them a fine run for their money, darting up a tree trunk at the last possible moment and even hanging upside-down just out of reach to chatter insults at the dog below. Gipsy scents a squirrel, or sees it in the distance, and immediately gives chase. Joanna, on the other hand, naturally 'points' – standing stock-still on sighting the squirrel and eventually stalking it very slowly until she is as close as she feels she can get. Then she will launch into the chase. She is much more cautious about this than her older friend but is not naturally cautious in other situations: Gipsy in fact is overall the more cautious of the two dogs, and Joanna the more inquisitive.

On the rare occasions when one of the spaniels actually catches a squirrel or a rabbit neither of them will savage it. They try to lift it gently and carry it off – a true characteristic of the spaniel family is a soft mouth. The danger in this gentle behaviour with squirrels (and many other small mammals) is that the poor spaniel gets a nasty bite for its pains – so keep an eye on such chases. We once discovered the presence of a family of rats beneath our rabbit hutches: Joanna barked and chased when we flushed them out and narrowly escaped being bitten by one she pinned to the ground.

Trifle, a cheerfully cooperative Clumber Spaniel puppy of fourteen weeks, takes his place to be photographed (Raycroft String of Pearls, owned by Mr & Mrs Whewell)

Most spaniels have similar soft mouths – and most have a remarkable scenting ability, being able to pick up scent trails and follow them for miles in the countryside. When I was quite young, in the Sussex countryside, I used to help an ancient retired farmer to look after his chickens, geese and ducks. He lived mostly on his own with a little help from his great-granddaughter Jenny and her Cocker Spaniel bitch Sophie. One evening when I called round to see that the fowls were shut up for the night, the old man and Jenny were very concerned because Sophie had apparently disappeared – not having been seen since early morning. I suggested setting out to search for her, since it was a sunny summer's evening, and took with me a Welsh Springer called Rush, who knew Sophie well and was, as they say in the country, 'a good nose'.

We let the Springer sniff Sophie's blanket before we set off and told him several times to 'find Sophie'. Although his ears pricked up at the sound of his friend's name he did not seem to get the hang of the search for some time. There was an old railway line a few fields away and we were searching along this calling Sophie, and whistling for her, when Rush suddenly stood stock-still and, with ears pricked and nostrils quivering, turned slowly round to face the direction of the slight breeze. Suddenly, with a series of short barks he took off, running for a small copse at the top of a hill a field and a half away. We followed as fast as we could and, on reaching the copse, we saw him standing wagging his tail and barking softly over Sophie, who was lying close to the entrance of a fox's earth. She had been trapped by one of her long ears in the cruel jaws of a gin-trap – a vicious barbed steel trap outlawed in England and Wales in 1958 – barbarously used for catching foxes as well as smaller mammals such as stoats and weasels. The ear was badly torn and it and one shoulder were bleeding, but the poor spaniel had finally tired of her struggles and lain down exhausted in the blood-soaked mud. She must have been sniffing around in the undergrowth and narrowly missed catching her face in the trap – luckily since she would almost certainly have died had she been more seriously caught and mutilated.

We carried Sophie back home, as she was quite weak and had lost a good deal of blood. The trap, in snapping shut, had grazed her shoulder with its teeth and clamped firmly right through the 'leather' of her ear. She needed several stitches and some days of rest. The ear healed over eventually, leaving a jagged side to it and she always looked a little lop-sided after this escapade. Rush, of course, was heartily congratulated and it was not just fancy to think that the two dogs were much firmer friends after Sophie's ordeal and Rush's great rescue operation.

Never pick up either a puppy or a full-grown dog without supporting its weight fully. A hand should go under its bottom and the other under its shoulders, taking the bulk of the weight on the hand supporting the bottom end. This is the best way to lift a dog – for examination on a table, for example, or when you are about to bathe it.

Nervousness and stress can be found in dogs just as in other creatures and several rules help to prevent it. Never pick up a puppy suddenly and never let children keep picking up a puppy. Also never leave a puppy alone for hours at a time in an unoccupied house. Gentle patience is also essential. Some nervousness may be due to inbreeding or can be hereditary, and you should look for signs of it when purchasing. However, nervousness in spaniels can be the result of incorrect (and often selfish) handling of puppies. A puppy should get used to the smell and feel of its owner's hands, and these hands should be gentle in order to give the puppy confidence and trust – reassuring it in a new and unknown world.

Grooming
Handling a dog with confidence will also pay dividends during grooming. Regular grooming is very necessary for spaniels and if they have been handled well in puppyhood and have become used to the gentle use of brush and comb, they will enjoy it. Grooming can start in early puppyhood, in fact as early as three weeks old – if the puppy will stay still long enough! Grooming does not consist merely of brushing and combing but, on a regular basis, should include attention to the eyes, ears, feet and mouth. It is ideal to groom a dog each day, and if you can do this your spaniel will always look superb. Dogs enjoy routine, and if they are groomed daily

they will look forward to it and thoroughly enjoy the attention. I once had a Cocker Spaniel who, if I forgot to groom her for a day or two, would fetch the brush she liked best, accompanying the act with the tail-and-rear-end wagging so characteristic of the breed. She enjoyed her ears being inspected and would even open her mouth, drawing her lips back to bare her teeth for me to look inside. She was a spaniel who masterminded her own life, acknowledging that I was the 'boss' but, through cunning feminine wiles, manoeuvring me into a situation from which I could not escape without too obviously making her sad. Yet should I have to leave her at home on her own, she seemed to understand and accepted the decision with good grace. If there was the slightest chance, however, that she might be taken on the trip, she seemed to sense it and would not let up on me until I had told her she could come. She was always admired because she was well behaved and spick and span (mostly due to her own efforts) – a typical 'merry' spaniel, anxious to please and attentive to what she considered to be her duties.

If I was out late at night, she would curl up just inside the door, awaiting my return. If I tried to enter quietly, without waking anyone, she seemed to understand the intention and to try to be part of the act, staying perfectly silent. The result was often a disaster, for once she had crept towards me in the dark and we had made contact, her enthusiasm combined with her wish to please and not make any noise resulted in her rolling around the hallway with excitement, so that she usually knocked over some piece of furniture or tripped me up on the way to the stairs!

Regular brushing and grooming prevents dandruff, discourages fleas and other parasites and frees the spaniel's coat of tangles acquired during a country walk or a roll in the garden. The best kind of brush is one with bristles on one side and metal teeth on the reverse. The bristles will do all brushing except the tangles, which require patient attention from the metal side. Spaniels will put up with any amount of untangling with the tough side of the brush, but on a dry dog a comb tends to pull too hard in delicate places and they object. If the brushing is regular enough – and includes all the less accessible places such as the armpits, undersides of ears

The head of an English Springer Spaniel shows its strength of character and appealing nature, which make it an ideal companion or working dog

and 'feathers' at the tail end – it usually gives good results. If a comb becomes necessary, use a steel one, and for your own convenience one with a handle. If you really want to give your spaniel's coat a sparkle and a final sheen, use a piece of velvet after brushing; such 'polishers' as soft chamois leather are sometimes recommended, but velvet produces the best result on a healthy well-brushed coat.

To remove the dead hair that collects in any dog coat, catch it between thumb and forefinger and gently jerk it away downwards along the body; or remove it during bathing.

Bathing

There is much dissension among spaniel owners and breeders about bathing. Some say it should be done regularly, others say it is overdone and is only needed when the dog is muddy. Personally I find that brushing can usually achieve cleanliness and I do not recommend frequent bathing, particularly in winter. Show breeders wash their dogs regularly, for the show, but two or three baths a year are enough for a pet spaniel unless – as spaniels do – it rolls in something smelly and unpleasant. Then a bath is essential, with a good dog (not human) shampoo. Eucalyptus oil (and sometimes tomato ketchup) rubbed into the smelly part of the coat before washing will help. There are some excellent dog shampoos available: use one, because the natural oils in a dog's coat are affected by soapy water and take several days to regain their strength.

A dog can be bathed before a meal but not for about three hours after one – and do not bathe your spaniel outside in cold weather. Do some untangling on its coat before immersing it in water – otherwise the tangles harden into knots, which are even more difficult to remove. Put a rubber mat on the floor of the sink or bath, or else the dog's feet will slip and it will become terrified. Have everything to hand around the bath, such as shampoo, towel, etc, since the spaniel will decide it is time to jump out if you reach away for something. A breeder once gave me a tip on bathing: smear the inside of the spaniel's ear-flap lightly with Vaseline before a bath, and do the same with the rim around the eyes. It helps to avoid the possibility of water in the eyes and insides of the ears – very important, especially for the inner ear which must be kept dry.

After soaking the dog, rub in the liquid shampoo as you would on your own hair, carefully avoiding the eyes and the insides of the ears. If you have a shower so much the better, but take care that the water is neither too hot nor too cold. Rinse the dog thoroughly after soaping and lift it out of the bath to be dried.

Use one towel for the dog's body, rubbing the coat as dry as possible, with special attention to the joints of the legs and the back, chest and abdomen. Use your second towel for drying around the eyes, the ear-flaps and the head. After towelling, give a final dry with a chamois leather. Some people use an electric hair-dryer, although some dogs dislike its noise and, generally, it does tend to make the hair rather brittle. Drying all over is essential after a bath, even between the toes, under the tail and around the genitals.

Subsequently the spaniel's coat should be lightly combed through and the dog kept at an even temperature (not running out in the garden on a cold day, for example) until thoroughly dry.

Extra care should be taken with bathing old dogs (who may need it fairly regularly due to general body odours) and delicate dogs. Bitches in season should not be bathed, nor should a sick dog.

Trimming and Clipping

After bathing your spaniel, you can set about trimming its coat. This need not require scissors, clippers or any other instrument if performed regularly, as you only take away the dead hair. An 'overgrown' dog who becomes tangled and matted will need clipping properly. Trimming, as opposed to clipping, can usually be done with the fingers: this is a knack which requires practice but, rather like milking a goat, is not impossible to learn! The 'dead' part of the coat can be extracted in several ways: by brushing and combing, and by 'plucking', using the finger and thumb (preferably after the dog has been bathed). A thin rubber glove will make the process easier, allowing you to get a grip on the dead hair, gently plucking it in the direction of the lay of the coat.

Snipping with scissors is sometimes necessary for the odd tangle (but show breeders will not have that done, since it is 'against the Kennel Club rules' and dogs would be penalised in a show if the coat was found to be cut). Curved scissors can be used for the hair between the toes (even in Kennel Club rules) and around the foot itself.

When trimming, commence at the back of the head and work systematically down the body, then down the neck and shoulders. A Number 6 steel comb is useful for combing the coat through first and during the operation. With the curlier-coated breeds of spaniel, 'hand' trimming can be a little more difficult, but again the use of a comb during the process aids its effectiveness.

Although a coat-trimming session takes some time, clipping or trimming a dog's coat yourself is better than taking the dog to a 'dog parlour'. It takes about two hours to clip a dog well – that is if you include playing with the dog in between, and keeping it happy – so most commercial dog-beauticians have to make their profit by having a fast turn-round. This is not the best way for the spaniel, and accounts for the reluctance of some dogs to go to the beautician a second time. Occasionally a dog is handled roughly and even ill-treated by a beautician, and it is useless having a trim and well-clipped dog that has been upset and made nervous. There are some good, caring people who clip dogs' coats, often doing it either as a hobby (for a little 'pin' money) or as a service at boarding kennels for owners leaving their dogs while on holiday.

Clipping (or 'stripping') dogs also requires practice, but it is worth taking the trouble to learn the technique. There are several books on the subject, and electric clippers cost between about £30 and £150. Various blades are available for the clippers, so that delicate places such as between the toes can be done. Great care should be taken, but in the long run it is more rewarding – both for owner and spaniel – if the task can be done at home. An 'overgrown' dog is much less perky as well as looking tatty, especially in the summer when coats should be shorter for comfort.

Dry baths – that is to say baths that use powder instead of water – are usually suggested for the removal of parasitic additions to the dog's coat. I have always found them practically useless and the danger of the powder getting into the eyes and ears (not to mention one's own lungs), especially when brushing out, is another reason to dislike them. There are occasions when a veterinary surgeon may prescribe them, but do not use them for general grooming and bathing.

Spaniels' nails need attention every month or so but they do wear down with regular exercise, especially if this includes running over stony paths, pavements or even garden paving-stones. In this case they need only a little filing down every few months. If the nails begin to curve over into a hook and cannot effectively be filed down, it is best to take the dog to a veterinary surgeon, at least the first time, to see how nail clipping is done. It has to be a careful process, since there is a vein running down the centre of the nail and cutting back too far will make it bleed badly.

Medical Checks

Occasionally a spaniel may have problems associated with its tail end: it may consistently rub its bottom along the ground or it may cry out and turn around on itself from time to time. While the former action may be due to the presence of worms, collectively these symptoms may mean that the two anal glands, situated one on either side of the anus, have become clogged or inflamed. In the wild state these glands were used to squirt a nasty-smelling liquid for scentmarking purposes. Since the dog was domesticated the glands (luckily for us all) have not been used and sometimes need attention. The offending waste matter can be gently squeezed out by pressing through a pad of lint or cotton wool. If the condition worsens and there is inflammation, then veterinary attention may be required as abscesses may result. A quick inspection of the dog's tail end during grooming will usually ensure that any problem of this nature can be attended to in its early stages.

The spaniel's mouth should be examined during the grooming session to make sure that the teeth are in good order and the gums are healthy. As the dog gets older, teeth may decay and need to be extracted by the vet, or at least scaled. Excessive salivation by a dog may indicate painful teeth and should be investigated quickly and veterinary advice sought.

Ears and eyes should be regularly examined too. Some people say that the spaniel is prone to canker of the ear, but most of this can be prevented by regular attention (see Chapter 12) and by keeping the inside of the ear dry.

Handling and grooming your spaniel should be an enjoyable task – both for the dog and for yourself. Spaniels love to be cared for and regular attention to their coat and 'person' will usually be accepted cheerfully. If they are handled regularly – gently and firmly – right from their puppy days, their enjoyment of the process will be ensured.

Care of an Old Dog

Elderly spaniels need extra care. A few hints may help you keep a dog happy and healthy in the last years of its life.

Adjust the dog's diet in its later years to two small meals rather than one large one each day – thus helping a slower digestion. A little egg-custard or milk and honey added to the meal, as well as extra vitamins, will also help, particularly in cold winter months; cod-liver oil, in small quantities, helps to 'insulate' the old dog against the cold.

Bad teeth should be attended to by the vet. In fact a veterinary check-up every three or four months helps to guard against any geriatric disorders creeping in.

Give that little more care when brushing and combing, since an older dog's skin is more tender and its muscles more twingy. In an elderly spaniel bitch watch out for gynaecological conditions, such as an extra-long season or more frequent seasons than usual. This could indicate uterine inflammation, which needs a vet's attention.

Damp, as well as infection, can cause kidney disorders in the elderly dog, so it should receive extra protection from this and be very carefully dried off after a walk. Exercise should be taken a little less strenuously, although as a dog gets older it will usually set its own pace.

The most important care you can give to an elderly dog is to make it feel as wanted as it has always been. If there are younger dogs around, make sure that it does not miss the attention it has been used to. Keep it happy and interested, as well as healthy, and it should live to a ripe old age.

Castration and Spaying

There is much difference of opinion on the matter of neutering dogs. Some vets suggest spaying any bitch as a puppy if she is not to breed. Some also recommend castration of the dog in early life. There are of course two sides to every question. My own views are opposed to neutering spaniels unless there is a special reason for it.

Sometimes vets point out that if bitches are spayed or dogs castrated, there will be no unwanted puppies. These views prevail in a less than perfect world, but I must assume that potential spaniel owners (or those that already have spaniels) who have read this far will have accepted that they have special responsibilities to see their animals do not stray around; then there is no reason to neuter a spaniel just as a precaution against unwanted litters. Others believe (again with justification) that tumours are less likely to occur in a spayed bitch than in an unspayed one which has never had a litter. But there is also some evidence that other complications caused by hormone imbalance (such as falling hair) can occur in spayed bitches. There is also the view that if gynaecological trouble occurs with an unspayed bitch as she gets older, she can then have a total hysterectomy at that time. There is of course more shock from such an operation in later life, but on balance I feel, if the owner is a responsible one as far as breeding is concerned, the bitch should be left alone until there are any signs of trouble which indicate the need for spaying.

Castrating dogs is, in my opinion, necessary only if the dog is aggressive or neurotic through excessive sexual desires (it is not necessarily a cure for aggressiveness in itself), or if you are keeping a dog with a bitch and you do not wish them to mate. Some dogs are a nuisance when they detect a bitch in season and then, for the protection of the dog itself as well as local bitches, it is probably best, after the agreement of your vet, to have it neutered.

Another reason for castration could be that a dog develops anti-social habits such as fouling the house when a bitch is in season nearby. This is very uncommon in spaniels but if it does happen then castration will cure it.

As an alternative form of male contraception, a dog can have a vasectomy. This operation does not diminish its sexual desire, but it does render it sterile after about a month from the operation.

8

Exercise and General Training

Exercise is important to all active dogs, and specially important to spaniels. They require fresh air, with time and space to run around – preferably in open country – with a variety of country scents to interest their keen sense of smell. As discussed earlier, this is not to say that they cannot be kept in the town; they will do well in a town situation so long as they can have plenty of exercise – in open fields, parks, woods, etc. Exercise for the spaniel is as important as good food, contributing to fine health, a well-toned body, shining coat, bright eyes, alertness and good carriage. Above all it contributes to interest, and an interested dog is usually a happy and healthy one.

Like feeding times, it should be part of a routine. The spaniel does not need many hours of exercise a day, and early morning and evening times are generally the best – particularly on hot summer days. Weather, apart from heat, does not worry the average spaniel; it still enjoys its walk, even in heavy rain. However, it should be well dried with a towel on its return home to avoid a chill. Only the sick dog and the small puppy should be left without regular exercise.

Just how much exercise depends on so many factors – firstly the dog itself; then whether it is a working dog or a pet; and of course your own time and facilities. I have known spaniels who have been with their masters all day and every day, accompanying them on their outside jobs, and have thriven on it, living to ripe old ages. I have known others, equally healthy and long-lived, who have had just an hour's good run regularly each morning and the odd outings during holidays and weekends. The fact remains that exercise is very much a part of the spaniel's daily life and should never be neglected, even for one day.

Never run a spaniel alongside a horse or bicycle; the dog

A Brittany Spaniel on the move (Puk des Pigenettes, owned by Mr Stanley Smith)

cannot pace itself, and the method is often injurious and also dangerous on a road. Exercise is more fun if the owner joins in – by throwing a ball or stick for example – or if there are other dogs around and the spaniel can join in their games. If you have more than one spaniel they will play together on a walk, chase rabbits, birds or squirrels and generally amuse themselves. Even so it does no harm to join in with them, especially if you have trained them to retrieve a ball or stick.

When running your spaniel in suburban woods and parks, try to look out for broken glass and other potentially dangerous bits of rubbish. Glass is one of the worst hazards a dog can encounter and could cripple it for life, or at best cause a serious wound which takes weeks of careful attention to cleanse and mend.

Roads, railway lines and motorways are obvious hazards. Never let a dog stray near any of them, however well-trained it may be. A well-trained dog will stand more chance than an untrained one dashing to the edge of a road, but you as its handler must keep an eye on it whenever you are out and be aware of the hazards it may encounter just round the corner. I remember once when my attention wandered from my dog for just too long. The lake near where we were walking was frozen at the edges and some way out into the water, but was thawing in the centre – potentially a very dangerous situation.

My younger spaniel was a puppy at the time and I was perhaps preoccupied with her when I suddenly noticed that Gipsy had chased a moorhen to the very edge of the lake. I whistled her to stop but I was too late – she rapidly followed the bird onto the ice and when it dived for the water at the other side of the ice, she too plunged in. She quickly realised her mistake and no doubt heard my frantic whistling and calling. By then it was too late, however, and despite her desperate struggles she could not clamber back onto the ice. Her front paws could find no foothold and she scrabbled, crying piteously for she was getting colder and colder in the freezing water. Unfortunately I cannot swim and I was as desperate – and as helpless – as the dog. I tried breaking the ice with rocks and with branches heaved from nearby trees, even waded in up to my waist to try to break it, but the water was deep and I could only crack the covering a few feet out, while Gipsy was at least twenty-five yards out. I kept shouting and calling her, praying that she would not get too weak and slip under the ice – and perhaps my prayers were answered: a young girl and her father came running up and the girl went in to the freezing water, breaking the ice with her fists as she swam until she was able to release Gipsy, who swam with her help back to the bank. The girl undoubtedly saved Gipsy and I shall always be extremely grateful to Kay Reynolds for this brave act.

I should have been more attentive to the dangers of a frozen lake – especially when I knew I could not swim! A spaniel, however well-trained, will become distracted by simple doggy pleasures – such as chasing a likely-looking moorhen. The dog cannot work out in advance the ramifications of such a foolhardy act – but you can!

Training your spaniel can be fun and helps to strengthen the bond between human and dog. In any case it is important that the dog is basically trained, since obedience may at some time save it from injury or worse – for example, when crossing a road.

House-training
Obviously every dog must be house-trained, and this is probably the first step in training, to be started right away

with a puppy. As spaniels are so anxious to please, it is usually effective quite quickly if you put in a lot of time. Puppies, like human babies, have little control over themselves in the early weeks of their lives, and you have to remember that as they wake up after a nap, they will want to urinate. If you are quick enough into the garden with it – what better chance to praise the puppy. The bewildered little creature will gradually catch on to the fact that all this praise has to do with a quick dash to the garden to relieve itself! Never scold a puppy for lapses it cannot avoid, but praise it for achievement. The puppy will in any case take a few days to get used to unfamiliar surroundings, in its new home away from its litter companions.

Lead-training

The first collar and lead for a spaniel puppy should be the cheapest you can find, light and narrow. When the puppy grows out of it, get a sturdier collar (though not a heavy one), and a lead which is strong enough for the size of the dog, and long enough to make walking a pleasure rather than a continual tug-of-war. It should stretch at least from your own knee to your shoulder.

The puppy should be trained to walk on the left side of its owner and to 'walk to heel' without straining forward all the time. Some puppies accept this quicker than others, but they should learn to walk properly when on a lead – otherwise walks will be tiresome for both dog and owner. Some trainers favour the use of the 'check' (choke) chain, but though it has much to recommend it for strong heavy dogs, such as German shepherds, I find that spaniels generally respond better to a collar and lead. Again, each dog is different. If a check chain is used, it should be a light one. The check is a metal chain with a ring at one end, on which the lead is fastened: as the dog pulls forward the chain becomes tighter, slackening when the dog is walking correctly. If the puppy dislikes it, change to a leather collar and lead.

In both the UK and the USA, the law demands that each dog wears a collar when out, bearing the owner's name and address. This is a sensible protection for your dog as well as you. Take off the collar indoors – it wears the hair on the dog's neck, and apart from this the puppy's pleasure at having a walk should be associated with putting on a collar and lead. In this way it quickly gets used to its collar and from there you can start its lead training.

About a quarter of an hour a day is enough for a puppy's early lead training in the garden. If it twists around and tugs you about like a big fish on the end of a line, gently bring it back to heel on your left side, holding the end of the lead in your right hand and having the lead across your body steadied by your left hand. Your left hand can control the dog's walking – gently but firmly. You can at first let the puppy trail the lead from its collar while you encourage it to follow you around if it is too boisterous, but the sooner the puppy gets used to its lead, the sooner it will be trained. Patience is again of the utmost importance; the puppy will have a sharp, retentive memory, but you must communicate that the training is a lesson and not a general rough-and-tumble. A puppy should not be allowed to walk too long, nor to strain against the lead, as that will affect the shape of the shoulders.

While on the lead the puppy should be trained to sit (on the edge of a kerb, for example) and wait until told to go. It must learn that the road is a dangerous place. A small tasty titbit may be a useful reward to various pieces of early training, though this is rarely essential so long as you are generous in your praises when the puppy is successful.

Further Training
Work out what additional training you plan to give the dog (this depends on whether the dog is working or a companion). Make a note of the various words of command you will use. It matters little what those words are, so long as you and anyone else who takes the dog out, can stick to them. A special whistle, for example, which the spaniel recognises (usually two tones is enough) should be repeated until the dog gets to know it.

Commands such as 'sit', 'stand', 'here', '(lie) down', 'stay', 'heel' and 'fetch' are prime examples of basic training, and should be called clearly and loudly – 'spat out' is a description one dog trainer gave me. Praise words are important too, and these should also generally be the same, such as '*what* a good dog' or 'good dog' accompanied by a session of making a fuss, stroking and gentling. The scolding – to be rapped or 'growled' out when the dog disobeys – can be 'naughty dog' or 'bad dog' or, as I use with my dogs, a short sharp growl from you – it works wonders. A growl from me (so long as they are within earshot – otherwise my throat suffers) is enough even to make them drop something they have picked up to eat on a walk!

Sometimes you may find that a spaniel responds to a word which is not really associated with the action. A farmer taught his spaniel all sorts of 'nonsense' words so that he alone could control it: to see it sit smartly down when he snapped 'rabbits' at it and return to him when he called 'scatter' was amusing, but the dog could not have cared less about the words; it was the sound to which it responded. This is why a command should be sharp and snappy – hissed, growled, barked or rapped out so that the dog cannot confuse it with another. My own younger spaniel bitch, Joanna, always responds to the command 'fetch' by running off and collecting whatever she is supposed to fetch, bringing it back and *dropping it* at my feet. I have never needed the command 'drop' with her, but have to use it with Gipsy. If other people order Joanna to 'drop it' she will not do so, just playing around with the object until the words 'fetch' or 'fetch it here' are used.

Your spaniel should also be taught to walk to heel without a lead, but I never risk doing this on roads where traffic is about, since however well-trained the dog there is always a chance that something will distract it, and then the dog's life is at stake. Only let the dog off the lead when well away from a road and it can run free in safety.

Much of a spaniel's training programme depends on the circumstances of its owner. If you have an estate car and put three dogs at once in the back, as I do, each should learn not to jump out willy-nilly as soon as the tailgate is opened. From experience, total chaos results when several dogs rush out in different directions. With a little training such an inconvenience – sometimes a dangerous one – can be avoided

If you are going to show your spaniel, it has some special

things to learn, discussed in the next chapter. For training the working spaniel, see Chapter 10.

When training a spaniel, consistent repetition brings the best results, and remember that your pupil is a dog and not a human being. It will respond as a dog, and needs praise every time it is successful. If it is unsuccessful do not praise it – merely repeat the exercise until it is correct, then shower the dog with praise and affection. It will soon get the message. With patience, gentleness, understanding and distinct commands, your spaniel will gradually (quite rapidly, in fact) become reasonably well-trained. It is up to you whether you require perfection in the form of parade-ground performance or a reliably trained, obedient dog and companion. Personally, I believe any dog should be trained within its own natural limits and I go for the second choice, but many owners will register horror at that. To some people the imposition of one's will on a dog is of the greatest importance – it reflects one's ability to command. But each spaniel has its own individuality and its own personality: crush those by over-training, and you will have a submissive (or neurotic) subordinate, not a true friend. I believe in developing the dog's personality by means of training – again, within its limits – getting it to do what it wants to do, and what you want it to do, once it knows right from wrong. As the dog gets to know you it will understand by the tone of the command, as well as the command itself, what it should do, how quickly – and how serious you are. What is most important to me is the association and bond between the spaniel and its owner, not the precision of its training. I like a spaniel that is happy as well as reasonably well-trained.

Shout at a spaniel only when you need to through distance; never hit it – unless you find that a sharp tap on the rump if it has really disobeyed or, in house-training, a tap on the rear with a rolled-up newspaper, has the desired effect. There is never any need to clout a naughty dog; doing that is usually a reflection of your own temper or frustration.

Jumping Up

A puppy should be trained not to jump up at people. Unfortunately, it is generally in a dog's nature to jump up, since it is often trying to put its nose on that of its owner in greeting! It may also be a form of curiosity, if the person it jumps up at is not known to it. Whatever the reason, having a dog, small or large, clean or muddy, jumping up at you can be not too welcome, especially to a stranger unprepared for the full force of a furry tornado all over his best suit. When I was in my teens a girlfriend, the daughter of a local farmer, invited me to lunch with her parents. I foolishly put on my best suit and, on arrival, was sent off to see her father who was working out in the cowsheds. As I turned the corner of the building three large, very muddy and typically eager Irish Water Spaniels rushed at me, jumping up to lick my face. In seconds I was plastered with mud, but the *coup de grâce* was delivered by the family's mastiff, who rushed up behind the spaniels and pinned me to the wall with his forepaws on my shoulders. There I had to stay until the commotion brought the farmer out; he merely smiled and said: 'I shouldn't let him do that if I were you – he's dirty.'

Train your dog, then, not to jump up at strangers, or indeed at anyone. The friendly dog finds it hard not to express enthusiasm in this way when greeting its owner, and I always go down to the dog's level when returning home and expecting a greeting from, in my house, several different directions. Indeed, if greeted boisterously by a dog, the best approach – providing it's small enough – is to stoop down and fuss the dog, allowing it to 'rub noses' and it will be happy. A friendly greeting with your own dog should not be thought a chore – it is an expression of the bond of friendship between dog and owner, in the dog's own terms. 'He rubs his nose on my tailored clothes, but I say not a word to that; for the good Lord knows, I can buy more clothes, but never a friend like that.'

Enjoying Training

I once had a Springer Spaniel dog which came to me after some ill-treatment at about a year old. He had obviously been well-trained for the gun but, I suspect, had been rejected by a perfectionist master, since he was always an eager, active dog who found it difficult to remain still in the face of running game. Not knowing all of the dog's background at the time, I took him out in the beautiful countryside of Windsor Great Park and at first he would often raise a pheasant and hesitate as it flew, watching me to gauge my reaction and probably waiting for me to shoot it. As I have no passion for killing creatures for sport, I let him go, half-encouraging him to chase the pheasant (which of course he had no chance of catching). He soon learnt, with evident joy, that his part in the partnership was not to wait while I shot his 'find' but to join in the hunt and chase. He was delighted and we became firm friends very quickly. He never lost the soft gentleness he had apparently learnt earlier in retrieving, and several times in his life brought abandoned leverets and baby rabbits to me gently in his mouth and laid them at my feet for attention, with much self-congratulation. His gentleness was a hallmark of his personality and only once, when I was attacked on a walk, did I witness a fierce fury, as he leapt to my defence. Once, when he nearly died from haemorrhagic gastro-enteritis, I sat with him continually for three days and three nights, and we both knew we had a special understanding between us. That understanding meant that his obedience was as much a mark of his respect as anything instilled in him by an early training. He merely adapted it to suit my own ways.

Remember that, while your spaniel may well be more stupid than you are overall, its emotional outlook is likely to be similar to your own. Dogs can become overstressed, just like their owners; can be happy and sad, worried, frightened, bewildered and angry. Such emotions need to be taken into account when attempting to communicate with your spaniel or to train it. It is thought that dogs cannot look to the future – they tend to live for the present, with some help from the past. For this reason they sometimes suffer unnecessarily and their emotional attitudes and feelings should always be considered. For example, if you are away for a few days a spaniel will probably suffer just as much in those days as if you had died, because it cannot rationally work out that you will soon be back again. This does not mean that your dog will pine away every time you go shopping without it – but it will certainly be happier when you come back!

Dogs should, in theory, be easier to train than any other

animal but some need more patience, perseverance and attention than others – because each one is different, emotionally, from another.

Never continue too long with a training session: if a dog becomes tired (or bored) its response will be affected. Never chastise or punish a dog unless you are sure that it understands *why* you are displeased. Warmth, kindness and affection always pay off in any training session – not only in ultimately successful training but in the development of understanding between owner and dog.

Tricks

My mind rebels against seeing a stately spaniel sitting up and begging for biscuits, rolling over to 'play dead' or walking on its hindlegs to obtain a morsel of a reward. It seems degrading, and although some dogs enjoy the attention they receive after successfully completing a 'trick' it seems better to train them to useful purpose – both for their own sakes and yours.

Some dogs, however, almost teach themselves to do something unusual. For instance a spaniel puppy I had when I was a boy had been taught by my father to fetch his and my carpet slippers from a cupboard. She was always delighted to do this and my father rewarded her each time with a dog biscuit. Eventually, if we were not sharp enough in requesting our slippers when we came home, she would rush off and bring them anyway, and if told that we did not need them, would charge back and forth with each shoe, boot or slipper she could find in the cupboard, grumbling and shaking each one furiously when being told to take it back! She was always a happy little dog, and even after she became blind, she would still insist on collecting our slippers from the cupboard, characteristically wagging her tail and rear end with great glee when she had completed the job successfully. She nearly always found the correct slippers for each person.

Training for the Countryside

While on the subject of exercise and training, a few words about the dog and the countryside are of importance. Whether or not you live in the country, you will know that

111

Joanna's coat shows the effects of the early morning dew

the merry spaniel is merriest if exercised in fields, woodlands or other natural places where it can pick up the scent of rabbits, squirrels, etc, and find an assortment of trails to follow. But there are points to remember (and to guard against) when giving a spaniel a run in the countryside.

First and foremost is to be aware of farming stock, and the possibility of your spaniel worrying sheep, cattle or even horses and donkeys. In any training programme, if possible include a session to teach the dog not to worry farm animals. Some people will say that their dogs would never be let out on the loose, and if they did get out they would not worry sheep anyway. But this *is* a risk; and it is also true that there are many people who have little consideration for the countryside and its inhabitants. Anyone reading this book and seriously considering teaming up with a spaniel must not be one of them!

Thoughtless people may be thoughtful too late – perhaps releasing a dog from a car in the country and letting it through a gateway into a field. The dog happily runs off and the first movement in sight is probably a flock of sheep – which start running away. The dog, untrained and knowing no better, finds fun in chasing them – and there the trouble starts. A dog which has 'got the idea' for chasing livestock will be very difficult to break. Some drastic measure may be necessary (if the dog is not quite legally shot by an angry farmer beforehand), such as to tether a sheep-worrying dog to a young ram: the result is harrowing for the dog though often successful. Please do not let such a procedure be necessary; if it is, then sheep have been needlessly worried, your dog has come close to being shot by a farmer and you will have a difficult dog as a companion.

Train your dog in advance. This can be done quite easily. Take it when a puppy to the countryside, and while it is safely on a lead, familiarise it with the smells and sight of livestock, telling it firmly 'no' if it wants to dash off from the footpath in the direction of sheep or cows. If the dog is properly trained to basic obedience standards it will respond immediately. Just make sure that the commands are given. A dog should always be brought to heel in the presence of farm stock and should learn to respect them very early in its life. It must learn to differentiate between the smells and sight of a rabbit, for example, and of a sheep. Never forget the importance of this lesson to your dog any more than its lesson in road drill.

Always remember the code of the countryside on your walks with your spaniels. If you open gates, close them afterwards; keep your dog in sight and bring it to heel if there is farm stock about; just as you yourself never walk through a field of crops, make sure your dog keeps to the edges of the field with you. As the proud owner of the best country dog of all, the spaniel, you will be one that respects the natural countryside, its inhabitants, guests and wildlife.

9

Showing and the Breed Standards

Showing spaniels can be an interesting, if time-consuming, pastime. Before going into the business of showing, be warned – it does take up much of your time and needs quite an investment in terms of travelling, show entrance-fees and some initial equipment. If you plan to breed spaniels professionally, of course, showing is important, for you will be able to sell your pups at a higher rate. If you have good dogs, it is useful to show them so that their best features and attributes do not go unrecognised. The two aspects go hand in hand. If the spaniel is a good one with all the desirable points, then breeding from it will help perpetuate the line; and the line will only be recognised as being of the best if awards are gained at recognised dog shows.

Entering
To enter a show, a spaniel must be six months old and be registered at the Kennel Club where it will be placed on the Active Register.

Small shows – known usually as 'Sanctioned and Limited' shows – often have a closing date of about three or four weeks before the show date, while for Open shows it is about four or five weeks in advance. Most Championship shows post a closing date of about six to eight weeks ahead. After sending your entry and the appropriate fee, you probably wait until about a week before the show when you receive your Exhibitor's Pass and the dog's catalogue number. Another form of dog show is the Exemption, which is often held in aid of charity. Many of the entries are inexperienced dogs (some of which can be extremely boisterous too), but it is good early experience for you and your spaniel. Details of shows are in the dog magazines, which can be ordered by your newsagent, or from the Kennel Club.

A description of the main classes at the Kennel Club Show – Crufts – will provide an indication of what the owner of a show spaniel is aiming at. Copies of the full set of Kennel Club regulations and definitions of classes can be obtained from the Kennel Club in the UK and the American Kennel Club in the USA (see Appendix 3).

Firstly there is the 'Special Puppy' Class which can be entered by dogs between six and twelve months of age. The 'Novice' class is for dogs which have not won a Challenge Certificate or three or more First Prizes at Open and Championship Shows. 'Special Junior' is for puppies between six and eighteen months of age, and the 'Tyro' class is for those which have not won a Challenge Certificate or five or more First Prizes at Open and Championship Shows.

A 'Special Yearling' class is available for dogs aged between six months and two years, an 'Undergraduate' for those which have not won a Challenge Certificate or three or more First Prizes at Championship Shows, and a 'Graduate' class for dogs that have not won four First Prizes. 'Postgraduate' classes can be entered by dogs that have not won five Firsts.

The three 'limit' classes include the 'Minor Limit' for dogs which have not won two Challenge Certificates or three or more First Prizes in all at Championship Shows in Minor, Mid Limit, Limit and Open Classes, confined to the breed. The 'Mid Limit' class is similar, as is the 'Limit' but, in the former, three Challenge Certificates and five Firsts are applicable, while in the latter three Challenge Certificates under three different judges or seven Firsts are mentioned.

The 'Open' class – as the name suggests – is for all dogs of the breeds for which the class is provided and which are eligible for entry at the Show, and the 'Special Open' is similarly regulated but confined to Members of an Association.

Field Trials are held for dogs which have won prizes, Awards of Honour, Diplomas of Merit, or Certificates of Merit in actual competition at a Field Trial held under Kennel Club or Irish Kennel Club Field Trial Rules and Regulations. Finally, a 'Special Working Trial' is held for dogs which have won prizes in actual competition at a Working Trial for Bloodhounds held under Kennel Club Rules and Regulations

116

and have qualified for entry at the Show in accordance with Crufts regulations.

These rules may change slightly at times, so purchase a copy of the applicable regulations and obtain details of the qualifications needed before entering your spaniel in a major show.

Shows can be good fun for both spaniel and owner, once you have overcome initial problems. You meet many friendly people in show-rings; you can also find that some bitchiness goes on – and in no way originating from female dogs! You occasionally hear of nasty tricks played on competitors in the show-ring, including 'nobbling' dogs to make them off-colour when being judged; even such fearful things as pricking the pads of a worthy competitor to make it lame before going into the ring. Such deranged deeds – especially vile since it is the dog who suffers – are rare, but are a warning that all show dogs should be protected at shows, as well as outside them, and should never be left alone during the long wait for their turn in the ring.

A show should be regarded as a sporting event, since even if your spaniel is exceptionally good to look at, it may not be placed. A sportsmanlike attitude to losing or winning is necessary.

Preparation

Much preparation for your spaniel is required beforehand. First and foremost the puppy must learn to be handled by strangers without being 'difficult', and then to walk loosely on a lead and to stand still on a table. These basic first steps should be followed by a series of 'ringcraft' lessons which are usually run locally by the nearest spaniel association or club.

Travelling may be one of the first problems, as shows are held all round the country. Your dog needs to travel well and to learn to sit when necessary in a travelling box or cage – that is, if it is one of the smaller varieties of spaniel. If you have no car, travelling is even more of a problem.

Before a dog goes into a show it needs to be in top form – fit and healthy with a glossy coat, bright and alert. If the spaniel's condition is good, on the night before the show you have to bathe it and give a detailed grooming.

Three Blenheim Cavalier King Charles Spaniels in their travelling cage just after arriving at an outside show (Highfetal Golden Lorelei, Anchordown Enigma at Highfetal and Highfetal Gentle Libertine, owned by Miss Faith Legh)

The feet of a Cocker Spaniel receive extra attention before entering the show-ring

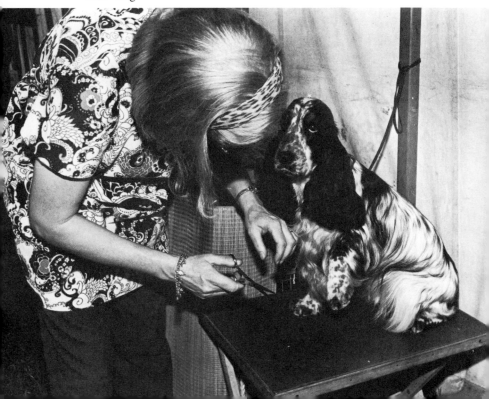

The first dog I ever took to a show was a Cocker bitch puppy. I had spent much time preparing her – listening to advice, reading all the little books giving tips on how to show a dog and carefully training her beforehand in dealing with strangers, being attentive to my commands and sitting and standing still, as well as walking to heel and other details. The great day came and the puppy and I set off for our first show, held outside at a County Show. We had high hopes, my spaniel and I. We waited (perhaps a little too impatiently), fidgeting with additional grooming and last-minute preparations. When our turn finally came to enter the ring I was far more nervous than the dog but this situation was to reverse itself very quickly. The first loud, crackling announcement over the loudspeaker coincided with a passing encounter with an Irish wolfhound, and my spaniel emitted a howl of fright, tugged her lead smartly out of my hand – and bolted! The pandemonium which followed was reminiscent of a Laurel and Hardy film – only in colour! We both went home a little shamefaced. But though it was a non-event as far as we were concerned, it was a good day with plenty of atmosphere (most of it around my spaniel and me, if I remember correctly), and it taught me, at least, a sound lesson: you must be *ready*, and so must your spaniel, when you go to your first show. I forgot that the one thing she had not encountered before was a loudspeaker. Familiarise your new show puppy with the atmosphere of the ring and the noises beforehand – as well as every other potential hazard – until it is used to it. Tape recordings of show noises can help.

When arriving at a show, check in with the Steward, and pin on your ring number before entering the ring. The judge will first look at the dog on a table and then watch it moving around. When standing, the dog should be squarely positioned with your fingers just tipping up its head. When moving around in front of the judge the lead should generally be slack. Walk the spaniel at the pace it finds most comfortable: some are better at a relatively fast pace, others slow. Occasionally you see owners at shows thundering along with their dogs as if pursued by the Hound of the Baskervilles in order to keep the lead slack; some limits need to be observed when training a show spaniel. Finally you both stand in line with the other competitors while the judge looks you all over once again – with your spaniel back in a good standing position. Those selected will be brought forward and the others will be dismissed by the Steward. If your dog is selected for further consideration, remember to keep it alert and standing well. If you are not lucky, then try again. Breeders and judges are helpful and quite ready to give advice if it is requested in a pleasant way. You can learn both from your own mistakes and from those around you, in and out of the show-ring. Gradually it will pay off, and if you really have a good specimen of spanielhood you will win through in the end.

Some people are very disorganised about going to shows and are forever needing to borrow things from those around them. The people who arrive with a travelling circus can be a nuisance, too, in shows where preparation space is limited, so use moderation in deciding what to take. A brush and comb are essential – elementary, but it is surprising how many amateurs of the ring forget one or the other; a paper kitchen-roll is useful for dog *and* handler; take a drinking bowl and a bottle of clean water in case a supply is not handy; one or two clean newspapers (to stand the dog on while preparing it); TCP and cotton wool; a clean dry towel; a small familiar rug in case your spaniel needs to curl up while waiting its turn; your show lead (and a spare); a small folding chair for yourself; a nail file. You may also need a little food for your dog and yourself, and a rubber mat or mattress to stand the spaniel on for its final grooming, so that it does not slip if the bench surface is shiny. For a smaller breed of spaniel you may also need a wire cage for travelling. These are usually foldable when not in use and quite light to carry. Some versions have a set of wheels for transporting around the show area rather like a shopping trolley. All your requirements (except the travelling cage and your chair) should be packed in a zipped bag with handles for carrying easily.

The Shows

Apart from dog shows of the type mentioned above, there are of course field trials and working trials. Their history in the

UK goes back to 1900. It was the policy of the Kennel Club Committee then to have as few rules and restrictions as possible, and shows were divided into three categories – recognised, licensed and sanctioned – provided the show executive entered an agreement to adopt the Kennel Club show regulations. Show guarantors conducted the shows (and still do) under these rules. From the thirty Championship shows scheduled in 1900, the annual number had grown to 2,881 by 1981, of which 453 were Championship shows. In the same year 289 Field Trials and Working Trials were held.

The best-known dog show in the UK is of course Crufts, founded by Charles Cruft, who worked as a traveller for James Spratt, selling a range of 'dog cakes'. Cruft had to visit the kennels of various sporting gentlemen throughout England and the Continent. Having promoted the dog section of the Paris Exhibition, and managed the Allied Terrier Club Show at Westminster in 1886, Cruft's own first show was held in 1891 at the Royal Agricultural Hall, Islington, North London; some ten years later it had become highly popular. No privately owned dog shows are now run and show licences are only granted by the Kennel Club to non-profit-making organisations. The widow of Charles Cruft (he died in 1938) eventually asked the Committee of the Kennel Club to take over the organisation of the event, and in 1948 the first Crufts show held under the auspices of the Kennel Club was staged at Olympia in London.

Crufts is now a three-day event and attracts an entry of about 10,000 dogs. One of the main features is the Obedience Championships, a competition between dogs which have obtained top honours at Championship Obedience Shows during the year. The Kennel Club has long encouraged obedience training and there are over 500 dog-training clubs in the UK registered with the Kennel Club, involving crossbred as well as purebred dogs.

In the USA apart from 'matches' – shows where dogs can compete in a show atmosphere without actually being in a show – there are five official show classes: the 'Puppy Class' is for dogs of six to twelve months of age that were born in the USA or Canada; the 'Novice Class' is for dogs of six months and over which have never won a prize other than in the

Puppy Class; the 'Bred by Exhibitor Class' is open to all dogs (except champions) of six months and older exhibited by their breeder or the immediate family, or by the kennels which bred them, as registered at the American Kennel Club; the 'American Bred Class' is open to all dogs of six months and older that were born in the USA after a mating in the USA; and the 'Open Class' is open to all dogs of six months or older, with no exceptions.

In addition there are 'Specials Only', brace and team and local classes, and 'Junior Showmanship' entries to allow children of different age groups to show dogs owned by their families. This useful encouragement to youngsters helps them become familiar with the show ring and also with the correct handling of dogs.

A very useful body in the USA for spaniel owners (and visitors) is the American Spaniel Club, based in New York. It holds an annual show each January in the New York City area for 'All Flushing Spaniels', and another event in July which moves around the United States and is for Cocker Spaniels only. The club sponsors field trials and each show has all regular classes, Junior Showmanship and Obedience trials. The club also introduced a 'Health Registry', which lists animals tested throughout the year and found free of congenital eye problems, blood-clotting abnormalities and hip dysplasia. The American Spaniel Club – formerly the American Cocker Spaniel Club – was formed in 1881 and claims to be the oldest organisation in the United States devoted to purebred dogs.

Spaniel standards in the USA are not always the same as those of the Kennel Club in England. The American Kennel Club does not, however, hold shows of its own generally, although it 'administers the sport of dogs'.

The Breed Standards
Below are reproduced (in alphabetical order) the spaniel standards of the British Kennel Club – similar to those of their American counterparts. However, in the USA there are some variations for dogs shown there and those interested in the fine detail of such variations should purchase the fairly extensive publication of the American Kennel Club (see

Appendix 3) that is devoted solely to the subject.

These 'standards of the breeds' are reproduced by kind permission of the Kennel Club of Great Britain.

AMERICAN COCKER SPANIEL

General Appearance A serviceable-looking dog with a refinedly chiselled head; standing on straight legs and well up at the shoulders; of compact body and wide, muscular quarters. The American Cocker Spaniel's sturdy body, powerful quarters and strong, well-boned legs show him to be a dog capable of considerable speed combined with great endurance. Above all he must be free and merry, sound, well balanced throughout, and in action show a keen inclination to work, equable in temperament with no suggestion of timidity.

Head and Skull Well developed and rounded with no tendency towards flatness, or pronounced roundness, of the crown (dome). The forehead smooth, ie free from wrinkles, the eyebrows and stop clearly defined. The median line distinctly marked and gradually disappearing until lost rather more than halfway up to the crown. The bony structure surrounding the socket of the eye should be well chiselled; there should be no suggestion of fullness under the eyes nor prominence in the cheeks which, like the sides of the muzzle, should present a smooth, clean-cut appearance. To attain a well-proportioned head, which above all should be in balance with the rest of the dog, the distance from the tip of the nose to the stop at a line drawn across the top of the muzzle between the front corners of the eyes, should approximate one-half the distance from the stop at this point up over the crown to the base of the skull. The muzzle should be broad and deep, with square, even jaws. The upper lid should be of sufficient depth to cover the lower jaw, presenting a square appearance. The nose of sufficient size to balance the muzzle and foreface, with well-developed nostrils and black in colour in the blacks and black-and-tans; in the reds, buffs, livers, and parti-colours and in the roans it may be black or brown, the darker colouring being preferable.

Mouth The teeth should be sound and regular and set at right angles to their respective jaws. The relation of the upper teeth to the lower should be that of scissors, with the inner surface of the upper in contact with the outer surface of the lower when the jaws are closed.

Eyes The eyeballs should be round and full and set in the surrounding tissue to look directly forward and give the eye a slightly almond-shape appearance. The eye should be neither weak nor goggled. The expression should be intelligent, alert, soft and appealing. The colour of the iris should be dark brown to black in the blacks, black and tans, buffs and creams, and in the darker shades of the parti-colours and roans. In the reds, dark hazel; in the livers, parti-colours, and roans of the lighter shades, not lighter than hazel, the darker the better.

Ears Lobular, set on a line no higher than the lower part of the eye, the leathers fine and extending to the nostrils, well clothed with long, silky, straight or wavy hair.

Neck The neck sufficiently long to allow the nose to reach the ground easily, muscular and free from pendulous 'throatiness'. It should rise strongly from the shoulders and arch slightly as it tapers to join the head.

Forequarters The shoulders deep, clean-cut and sloping without protrusion and so set that the upper point of the withers is at an angle which permits a wide spring of rib. Forelegs straight, strongly boned and muscular and set close to the body well under the scapulae. The elbows well let down and turning neither in nor out. The pasterns short and strong.

Body Its height at the withers should approximate the length from the withers to the set-on of tail. The chest deep, its lowest point no higher than the elbows, its front sufficiently wide for adequate heart and lung space, yet not so wide as to interfere with straight forward movement of the forelegs. Ribs deep and well-sprung throughout. Body short in the couplings and flank, with its depth at the flank somewhat less than at the last rib. Back strong and sloping evenly and slightly downward from the withers to the set-on of tail. Hips wide with quarters well rounded and muscular. The body should appear short, compact and firmly knit together, giving the impression of strength.

Hindquarters The hind legs should be strongly boned and muscled with good angulation at the stifle and powerful, clearly defined thighs. The stifle joint should be strong and there should be no slippage in motion or when standing. The hocks should be strong, well let down and when viewed from behind, the hind legs should be parallel when in motion and at rest.

Feet Feet compact, not spreading, round and firm, with deep, strong, tough pads and hair between the toes; they should turn neither in nor out.

Gait The American Cocker Spaniel possesses a typical sporting dog gait. Prerequisite to good movement is balance between the fore and hind quarters. He drives with his strong powerful rear quarters and is properly constructed to the shoulder and forelegs so that he can reach forward without constriction in a full stride to counter-balance the driving force of the rear. Above all, his gait is co-ordinated, smooth and effortless. The dog must cover ground with his action and excessive animation should never be mistaken for proper gait.

Tail The docked tail should be set on and carried on a line with the topline of the back, or slightly higher; never straight up like a terrier and never so low as to indicate timidity. When the dog is in motion the action should be merry.

Coat On the head, short and fine; on the body, medium length, with enough undercoating to give protection. The ears, chest, abdomen, and legs should be well feathered, but not so excessively as to hide the American Cocker Spaniel's true lines and movement or affect his appearance and function as a sporting dog. The texture is most important. The coat should be silky, flat or slightly wavy, and of a texture which permits easy care. Excessive or curly or cottony texture coat should be penalised.

Colour Blacks should be jet black; shadings of brown or liver in the sheen of the coat are not desirable. Black and tan (classified under solid colours) should have definite tan markings on a jet black body. The tan markings should be distinct and plainly visible and the colour of the tan may be from the lightest cream to the darkest red colour. The amount of tan markings should be restricted to ten per cent or less of the colour of the specimen; tan markings in excess of ten per cent should be penalised. Tan markings which are not readily visible in the ring or the absence of tan markings in any of the specified locations should be penalised. The tan markings should be located as follows: —

1 A clear spot over each eye
2 On the sides of the muzzle and on the cheeks
3 On the underside of the ears
4 On all feet and legs
5 Under the tail
6 On the chest, optional, presence or absence should not be penalised.

Tan on the muzzle which extends upwards over and joins should be penalised.

Any solid colour other than black should be of uniform shade. Lighter colouring of the feathering is permissible.

In all the above solid colours a small amount of white on chest and throat, while not desirable, is allowed, but white in any other location should be penalised.

Parti-colours Two or more definite colours appearing in clearly defined markings are essential. Primary colour which is ninety percent or more should be penalised; secondary colour or colours which are limited solely to one location should also be penalised. Roans are classified as parti-colours and may be of any of the usual roaning patterns. Tri-colours are any of the above colours combined with tan markings. It is preferable that the tan markings be located in the same pattern as for black and tan.

Size The ideal height at the withers for an adult dog is 38cm (15 inches) and for an adult bitch 35cm (14 inches). Height may vary 1.3cm (half an inch) above or below this ideal. A dog whose height exceeds 39cm (15½ inches) or a bitch whose height exceeds 37cm (14½ inches) should be penalised. An adult dog whose height is less than 37cm (14½ inches) or an adult bitch whose height is less than 34cm (13½ inches) should be penalised. Note: Height is determined by a line perpendicular to the ground from the top of the shoulder blades, the dog standing naturally with its forelegs and the lower hind legs parallel to the line of the measurement.

Note Male animals should have two apparently normal testicles fully descended into the scrotum.

BRITTANY SPANIEL

The following standard for the Brittany Spaniel is the modern French Breed Standard, translated from the Club de L'Epagneul Breton 1981 (for which I am indebted to Stanley Smith of Rainham, Kent).

General Appearance Height: maximum 51cms (19.89 inches) minimum 46cms (17.94 inches). Ideal height for males 48–50cm (18.72 inches–19.50 inches) and for bitches 47–49cm (18.33–19.11 inches). The ideal weights are: 15 kilograms (33.07 pounds) for males and 13 kilograms (28.66 pounds) for bitches.

A compact dog, ears short and set high, skull rounded with tight lips, coat flat, lightly fringed, fringes wavy never curly, cobby type, tail never more than 10cms (3.9 inches) long; natural bob tail permitted.

Nose Darkish-coloured according to whether the dog is orange/white, liver/white, black/white or tri-coloured. Nostrils open, well shaped. Faults: bare nose patches (butterfly nose), too light nostrils that interfere with scenting.

Lips Tight with upper lip slightly overlapping the lower. Faults: too long or too short.

Muzzle Medium length, about two thirds the length of the skull. Faults: too long or too short.

Skull Medium length, rounded median line slightly marked. Well defined but not exaggerated stop. Faults: apple headed, distinct occipital crest, narrow or coarse. Stop heavily indented.

Eyes Brown, in harmony with the coat, lively and expressive. Faults: too light, mean, or bird-of-prey eyes.

Ears Set high, rather short, lightly fringed, though the ear ought to be well covered with hair. Leaf-shaped. Faults: low set, pendulous, too large, or with very curly hair.

Neck Medium length, well set on the shoulders, without dewlap. Faults: too long, too slender, too short and thick set.

Shoulders Oblique and well muscled. Faults; too straight or too angulated.

Forelegs Muscled, bony. Faults: bone too heavy or light.

Chest Deep, descending to the level of the elbow, sides well rounded, deep as well as wide. Faults: narrow, not deep enough, slab sided.

Back Short, withers well defined, never sway-backed. Faults: too long or sway.

Loins Short and strong. Faults: long and weak.

Croup Slightly falling. Faults: too straight or too steep.

Flanks Well rounded without excess. Faults: fat and falling.

Tail Level, docked if the dog does not have a natural short tail, always short, no more than 10cms (3.9 inches) often with a little twist, and ending with a queue of hair. Faults: long or bare.

Forelegs Very straight, with pasterns slightly bent, clean and muscled. Faults: pasterns too straight or falling radically, lack of feathering (elbow to pasterns)

Hindlegs Strong thighs, stifles well bent, muscular, not cowhocked. Thighs well feathered half way to the hock. Hocks short, not too bent. Faults: straight stifles, lack of feathering, too straight (hocks) or too bent.

Feet Toes compact with a little hair between. Faults: large, long, cat-footed, splayed.

Coat Flat, or slightly wavy, not excessively heavy. Faults: curly or too soft.

Colour Orange and white, liver and white, black and white, tri-colour, or roan or any of these colours.

Summary Thickset and strong backed. An elegant little dog, very vigorous in its movements, energetic, with an intelligent look, presenting the appearance of a full-blooded dog.

The judges should excuse, without prizes, all dogs under 46cm (18 inches) or over 51cm (20 inches).

Lack of pigment is a fault on the nose. Lack of pigment is a serious fault and no dog having a lack of it should receive a rating of excellent. If the lack of pigment is very minor, the dog may receive a rating of very good.

Monorchids may not be shown in dog shows or compete in Field Trials.

The classes in a show will be in two divisions: orange and white (1) and other colours (2).

CAVALIER KING CHARLES SPANIEL

General Appearance   An active, graceful and well-balanced dog. Absolutely fearless and sporting in character and very gay and free in action.

Head and Skull   Head almost flat between the ears, without dome. Stop shallow. Length from base of stop to tip about 3.8cm (1½ inches). Nostrils should be well developed and the pigment black. Muzzle well tapered. Lips well-covering but not hound-like. Face should be well filled out underneath the eyes. Any tendency to appear 'snipy' is undesirable.

Eyes   Large, dark and round but not prominent. The eyes should be spaced well apart.

Ears   Long and set high with plenty of feather.

Mouth   Level; scissor bite preferred.

Neck   Moderate length – slightly arched.

Forequarters   Shoulders well laid back; legs moderate bone and straight.

Body   Short-coupled with plenty of spring of rib. Back level. Chest moderate leaving ample heart room.

Hindquarters   Legs with moderate bone; well-turned stifle – no tendency to cow or sickle hocks.

Feet   Compact, cushioned and well-feathered.

Tail   The docking of tails is optional. No more than one-third to be removed. The length of the tail should be in balance with the body.

Coat   Long, silky and free from curl. A slight wave is permissible. There should be plenty of feather.

Colour   The only recognised colours are: Black and tan: Raven black with tan markings above the eyes, on cheeks, inside ears, on chest and legs and underside of tail. The tan should be bright. Ruby: Whole coloured rich red. Blenheim: Rich chestnut marking well broken up on a pearly white ground. The markings should be evenly divided on the head, leaving room between the ears for the much valued lozenge mark or spot (a unique characteristic of the breed). Tricolour: Black and white well spaced and broken up, with tan markings over the eyes, on cheeks, inside ears, inside legs and on underside of tail. Any other colour or combination of colours is most undesirable.

Weight and Size Weight 5.4–8.2 kilograms (12–18 pounds). A small well-balanced dog well within these weights is desirable.

Faults Light eyes. Undershot and crooked mouths and pig jaws. White marks on whole-coloured specimens. Coarseness of type. Putty noses. Flesh marks. Nervousness.

Note Male animals should have two apparently normal testicles fully descended into the scrotum.

CLUMBER SPANIEL

General Appearance That of a dog with a thoughtful expression, very massive but active, which moves with a rolling gait characteristic of the breed.

Head and Skull Head large, square and massive, of medium length, broad on top, with a decided occiput; heavy brows with a deep stop; heavy muzzle, with well-developed flew, and level jaw and mouth. Nose square and flesh-coloured.

Eyes Dark amber, slightly sunk with some haw showing.

Ears Large, vine-leaf shaped, and well covered with straight hair, and hanging slightly forward, the feather not to extend below the leather.

Mouth Should be level and neither over- nor undershot.

Neck Fairly long, thick and powerful, and well feathered underneath.

Forequarters Shoulders strong, sloping and muscular; chest deep. Legs short, straight, thick and strong.

Body Long and heavy, and near the ground, with well-sprung ribs. Back straight, broad and long.

Hindquarters Very powerful and well developed. Loin powerful, well let down in flank. Hocks low, stifles well bent and set straight.

Feet Large and round, well covered with hair.

Tail Set low, well feathered, and carried about level with the back.

Coat Abundant, close, silky, straight; legs well feathered.

Colour Plain white, with lemon markings, orange permissible; slight head markings and freckled muzzle, with white body preferred.

Weight and Size Dogs about 25–31.8 kilograms (55–70 pounds); Bitches about 20.4–27.2 kilograms (45–60 pounds).

Note Male animals should have two apparently normal testicles fully descended into the scrotum.

COCKER SPANIEL

General Appearance That of a merry, sturdy, sporting dog. The Cocker Spaniel should be well balanced and compact and should measure about the same from the withers to the ground as from the withers to the root of the tail.

Head and Skull There should be a good square muzzle with a distinct stop which should be mid way between the tip of the nose and the occiput. The skull should be well developed, cleanly chiselled, neither too fine nor too coarse. The cheek bones should not be prominent. The nose should be sufficiently wide to allow for the acute scenting power of this breed.

Eyes The eyes should be full but not prominent, brown or dark brown in colour but never light, with a general expression of intelligence and gentleness though decidedly wide awake, bright and merry. The rims should be tight.

Ears Lobular, set on low, on a level with the eyes, with fine leathers which extend to but not beyond the tip of the nose; well clothed with long silky hair which should be straight.

Mouth Jaws should be strong and teeth should have a scissor bite.

Neck Neck should be moderate in length, clean in throat, muscular and neatly set in fine sloping shoulders.

Forequarters The shoulders should be sloping and fine, the chest well developed and the brisket deep, neither too wide nor too narrow in front. The legs must be well boned, feathered and straight and should be sufficiently short for concentrated power but not too short to interfere with the tremendous exertions expected from this grand little sporting dog.

Body Body should be immensely strong and compact for the size and weight of the dog. The ribs should be well sprung behind the shoulder blades, the loin short, wide and strong, with a firm topline gently sloping downwards to the tail.

Hindquarters Hindquarters should be wide, well rounded and very muscular. The legs must be well boned, feathered above the hock with a good bend of stifle and short below the hock allowing for plenty of drive.

Feet Feet should be firm, thickly padded and catlike.

Tail Tail should be set on slightly lower than the line of the back; it must be merry, carried in line with the back and never cocked up. The tail should not be docked too long nor too short to interfere with its merry action.

Coat Flat and silky in texture, never wiry or wavy, with sufficient feather; not too profuse and never curly.

Colour Various. In self colours no white is allowed except on the chest.

Gait There should be true through action both fore and aft, with great drive covering the ground well.

Weight and Size The weight should be about 12.7–14.5 kilograms (28–32 pounds). The height at the withers should be approximately 38–39cm (15–15½ inches) for bitches and approximately 39–41cm (15½–16 inches) for dogs.

Faults Light bone; straight shoulder; flat ribs; unsound movement; weak hocks; weak pasterns; open or large feet; frown; small beady eyes; undershot or overshot mouth; uncertain or aggressive temperament.

Note Male animals should have two apparently normal testicles fully descended into the scrotum.

ENGLISH SPRINGER SPANIEL

Characteristics The English Springer is the oldest of our sporting gundogs and the taproot from which all of our sporting land spaniels (Clumbers excepted) have been evolved. It was originally used for the purpose of finding and springing game for the net, falcon, or greyhound, but at the present time it is used entirely to find, flush, and retrieve game for the gun. The breed is of ancient and pure origin, and should be kept as such.

General Appearance The general appearance of the modern Springer is that of a symmetrical, compact, strong, upstanding, merry and active dog, built for endurance and activity. He is the highest on the leg and raciest in build of all British land spaniels.

Head and Skull The skull should be of medium length and fairly broad and slightly rounded, rising from the foreface, making a brow or stop, divided by a fluting between the eyes gradually dying away along the forehead towards the occiput bone, which should not be peaked. The cheeks should be flat, that is not rounded or full. The foreface should be of proportionate length to the skull, fairly broad and deep without being coarse, well chiselled below the eyes, fairly deep and square in flew, but not exaggerated to such an extent as would interfere with comfort when retrieving. Nostrils well developed.

Eyes The eyes should be neither too full nor too small but of medium size, not prominent nor sunken but well set in (not showing haw) of an alert, kind expression. A mouse-like eye without expression is objectionable, as also is a light eye. The colour should be dark hazel.

Ears The ears should be lobular in shape, set close to the head, of good length and width, but not exaggerated. The correct set should be in line with the eye.

Mouth The jaws should be strong, with a perfect regular and complete scissor bite, ie the upper teeth closely over-lapping the lower teeth and set square to the jaws.

Neck The neck should be strong and muscular, of nice length and free from throatiness, well set in the shoulders, nicely arched and tapering towards the head – thus giving great activity and speed. An ewe neck is objectionable.

Forequarters The forelegs should be straight and nicely feathered, elbows set well to body and with proportionate substance to carry the body. Strong flexible pasterns.

Body The body should be strong and of proportionate length, neither too long nor too short, the chest deep and well developed with plenty of heart and lung room, well sprung ribs, loin muscular and strong with slight arch, and well coupled, and thighs broad and muscular and well developed.

Hindquarters The hindlegs should be well let down from hip to hocks. Stifles and hocks moderately bent, inclining neither inwards nor outwards. Coarseness of hocks is objectionable.

133

Feet   Feet tight, compact, and well rounded with strong full pads.

Gait   The Springer's gait is strictly his own. His forelegs should swing straight forward from the shoulder, throwing the feet well forward in an easy and free manner. His hocks should drive well under his body, following in a line with the forelegs. At slow movements many Springers have a pacing stride typical of the breed.

Tail   The stern should be low and never carried above the level of the back, well feathered and with a lively action.

Coat   The coat should be close, straight and weather resisting without being coarse.

Colour   Any recognised land spaniel colour is acceptable, but liver and white, black and white, or either of these colours with tan markings preferred.

Weight and Size   The approximate height should be 51cm (20 inches). The approximate weight should be 22.7kg (50lbs).

Note   Male animals should have two apparently normal testicles fully descended into the scrotum.

FIELD SPANIEL

General Appearance   That of a well-balanced, noble, upstanding, sporting dog; built for activity and endurance; a combination of beauty and utility; of unusual docility.

Head and Skull   The head should be characteristic as is that of the Bulldog or the Bloodhound; its very stamp and countenance should at once convey the impression of high breeding, character and nobility; skull well developed, with a distinct occipital protuberance, which gives the character alluded to; not too wide across the muzzle, long and lean, neither snipy nor squarely cut, and in profile curving gradually from nose to throat; lean beneath the eyes, a thickness here gives coarseness to the whole head. The great length of muzzle gives surface for the free development of the olfactory nerve, and thus secures the highest possible scenting powers. Nose well developed, good with open nostrils.

Eyes   Not too full, but not small, receding or overhung. The colour in all cases to match the coat and markings, except

134

in livers which may be a light hazel. Grave in expression suggesting docility and intelligence and showing no haw.

Ears Moderately long and wide, sufficiently clad with nice Setter-like feather and set low. They should fall in graceful folds, the lower parts curling inwards and backwards.

Mouth The jaws should be strong, with a perfect regular and complete scissor bite ie, the upper teeth closely over-lapping the lower teeth and set square to the jaws.

Neck Long, strong and muscular, so as to enable the dog to retrieve his game without undue fatigue.

Forequarters The shoulders should be long and sloping and well set back, thus giving great activity and speed. The foreleg should be of fairly good length, with straight, clean, flat bone and nicely feathered. Immense bone is not desirable.

Body Should be of moderate length, well ribbed up to a good strong loin, straight or slightly arched, never slack. The chest, deep and well developed, but not too round and wide. Back and loins very strong and muscular.

Hindquarters Strong and muscular. The stifles should be moderately bent and not twisted either in or out.

Feet Not too small, round with short, soft hair between the toes; good, strong pads.

Tail Well set on and carried low, if possible below the level of the back, in a straight line or with a slight downward inclination, never elevated above the back, and in action always kept low, nicely fringed with wavy feather of silky texture.

Coat Flat or slightly waved, and never curled. Sufficiently dense to resist the weather and not too short. Silky in texture, glossy and refined without duffelness, curliness or wiriness. On the chest, under the belly and behind the legs, there should be abundant feather, but never too much, especially below the hocks, and that of the right sort – viz, Setter-like.

Colour The Field Spaniel should be a self-coloured dog, viz: Black, Liver, Golden Liver, Mahogany Red, Roan; or any of these colours with Tan over the eyes, on the cheeks, feet and pasterns. Other colours, such as Black and White, Liver and White, Red or Orange and White, etc, while not debarring a dog, are a fault.

Weight and Size From about 16–23 kilograms (35–50½

pounds). Height: about 46cm (18 inches) at shoulder.

Faults Any departure from the foregoing points should be considered a fault and the seriousness with which the fault is regarded should be in exact proportion to its degree.

Note Male animals should have two apparently normal testicles fully descended into the scrotum.

IRISH WATER SPANIEL

Characteristics The gait, peculiar to the breed, differs from that of any other variety of Spaniel.

General Appearance The Irish Water Spaniel is a gundog bred for work in all types of shooting, and particularly suited for wild-fowling. His fitness for this purpose should be evident in his appearance; he is a strongly built, compact dog, intelligent, enduring and eager.

Head and Skull The head should be of good size. The skull high in dome, of good length and width sufficient to allow adequate brain capacity. The muzzle long, strong and somewhat square with a gradual stop. The face should be smooth and the skull covered with long curls in the form of a pronounced topknot growing in a well-defined peak to a point between the eyes. Nose large and well developed, dark liver colour. Withal there should be an impression of fineness.

Eyes Comparatively small, medium to dark-brown colour, bright and alert.

Ears Very long and lobe-shaped in the leather, low set, hanging close to the cheeks and covered with long twisted curls of live hair.

Mouth The jaws should be strong, with a perfect regular and complete scissor bite, ie, the upper teeth closely overlapping the lower teeth and set square to the jaws.

Neck Strongly set into the shoulders, powerful, arching and long enough to carry the head well above the level of the back. The back and sides of the neck should be covered with curls similar to those on the body. The throat should be smooth, the smooth hair forming a V-shaped patch from the back of the lower jaw to the breast bone.

Forequarters The shoulders should be powerful and sloping. The chest deep and of large girth with ribs so well sprung behind the shoulders as to give a barrel-shaped appearance to the body but with normal width and curvature between the forelegs. The forelegs should be well boned and straight, with arms well let down and carrying the forearm at elbow and knee in a straight line with the point of the shoulder.

Body Should be of good size. The back short, broad and level, strongly coupled to the hind quarters. The ribs carried well back. The loins deep and wide. The body as a whole being so proportioned as to give a barrel-shaped appearance accentuated by the springing of the ribs.

Hindquarters Powerful with long well-bent stifles and hocks set low.

Feet Should be large and somewhat round and spreading; well-covered with hair over and between the toes.

Tail Peculiar to the breed, should be short and straight, thick at the root and tapering to a fine point. It should be low set, carried straight and below the level of the back; and in length should not reach the hock joint. Three to four inches of the tail at the root should be covered by close curls which stop abruptly, the remainder should be bare or covered by straight fine hairs.

Coat Should be composed of dense, tight, crisp ringlets free from wooliness. The hair should have a natural oiliness. The forelegs covered with feather in curls or ringlets down to the feet. The feather should be abundant all round, though shorter in front so as only to give a rough appearance. Below the hocks and hindlegs should be smooth in front, but feathered behind down to the feet.

Colour A rich dark liver having the purplish tint or bloom peculiar to the breed and sometimes referred to as puce-liver.

Size Height to the shoulders: Dogs about 53–59cm (21–23 inches); Bitches about 51–56cm (20–22 inches).

Note Male animals should have two apparently normal testicles fully descended into the scrotum.

KING CHARLES SPANIEL

General Appearance Compact and cobby, on refined lines,

137

chest wide and deep, legs short and straight, back short and level. Tail well flagged, and not carried over the level of the back. Movement free, active and elegant.

Head and Skull Skull massive in comparison to size, well domed and full over the eyes. Nose black with large wide open nostrils, very short and turned up to meet the skull. The stop between skull and nose should be well defined. Jaw: muzzle square, wide, and deep and well turned up, lower jaw wide, lips exactly meeting, giving a nice finish.

The cheeks should not fall away under the eyes, but be well cushioned up. A protruding tongue is objectionable, but does not disqualify.

Eyes Very large and dark, set wide apart, with eyelids block square to face line, and with pleasing expression.

Ears Set on low, and to hang quite flat to cheeks, very long and well feathered.

Coat Long, silky and straight, a slight wave allowed, not curly, The legs, ears and tail should be profusely feathered.

Colour Black and tan: A rich glossy black, with bright mahogany tan markings on muzzle, legs, chest, linings of ears, under tail, and spots over eyes. Tri-colour: Ground pearly white and well distributed black patches, brilliant tan markings on cheeks, linings of ears, under tail, and spots over the eyes. A wide white blaze between the eyes, and up the forehead. Blenheim: A ground of pearly white with well distributed chestnut red patches. A wide clear blaze with the 'spot' in centre of skull. The 'spot' should be a clear chestnut red mark about the size of a sixpence in centre of skull. Ruby: Whole coloured, a rich chestnut red.

Weight and Size The most desirable size is 3.6–6.3 kilograms (8–14 pounds).

Faults The presence of a few white hairs on the chest of a Black and Tan or Ruby is undesirable, but a white patch is a major fault.

Note Male animals should have two apparently normal testicles fully descended into the scrotum.

PAPILLON (BUTTERFLY SPANIEL)

General Appearance This dainty balanced little toy dog

138

should have an attractive head, an alert bearing and an intelligent and lively expression. Movement should be sound, light and free and not cramped or restricted in any way.

Head and Skull The skull slightly rounded between the ears, the muzzle finely pointed and abruptly thinner than the skull accentuating the stop which should be well defined. Length from tip of the nose to the stop approximately a third length of the head. Nose should be black. Faults: Muzzle over long or coarse. Skull flat or apple shaped. Nose other than black.

Eyes Of medium size, rounded, dark in colour, placed rather low in the head and should not bulge. Faults: Eyes light in colour, too small or too large or protruding.

Ears The ears should be large and mobile with rounded tips, heavily fringed, set towards the back of the head far enough apart to show the slightly rounded shape of the skull. The ears must be completely erect or dropped. When the ears are erect they must be carried obliquely like the spread wings of a butterfly, therefore the name, Papillon. When the ears are dropped they must be completely dropped, and this type is known as the Phalene (moth). Faults: Semi-erect or not fully dropped, small sharply pointed or set too close together.

Mouth Scissor bite, upper teeth fitting close over lower. The lips thin and tight. Faults: Over- or undershot to the extent that the incisors do not touch at all. Wry mouth.

Neck Of medium length.

Forequarters Shoulders well developed and sloping back. Chest rather deep. Forelegs straight and slender and fine boned. Faults: Shoulders straight. Out at elbow.

Body Level topline. The body should have plenty of length, well formed with well sprung ribs, good length of loin which must not be weak, with slightly arched belly. Faults: Topline roached, dipped or cobby. Legs malformed and crooked, cow-hocked, too long or too short. Stifles straight, coupled with weak hindquarters.

Hindquarters Well developed, good turn of stifle. Legs when viewed from behind should be parallel. Dew claws on the hind legs must be removed.

Feet Fine and fairly long as in the hare. The tufts of hair between the toes extending far beyond them.

139

Tail Long and well fringed, set on high, arched over the back with the fringes falling to the side to form the plume. Faults: Tail unduly short, too low set.

Coat Should be abundant, flowing, but without undercoat, long, fine, silky, falling flat on back and sides forming a profuse frill on the chest, short and close on the skull, muzzle and front part of the legs. Back part of the front legs to pasterns, tail and thighs covered with long hair. Faults: Harsh, curly or stand-off coat.

Colour White with patches which may be any colour except liver. A tricolour must be black and white with tan spots over the eyes, tan inside ears and under root of tail and on cheeks. The head marking should be symmetrical about a white, narrow, clearly defined blaze.

Size The ideal height at the withers from 20.3–28cm (8–11 inches). The dog will appear to be slightly longer than high when properly furnished with ruff and hind fringes.

Faults Muzzle over-long or coarse. Skull flat or apple shaped. Nose other than black. Eyes light in colour, too small or too large or protruding. Ears semi-erect or not fully dropped, small, sharply pointed or set too close together. Mouth over or undershot to the extent that the incisors do not touch at all. Wry mouth. Shoulders straight. Out at elbow. Topline roached, dipped or cobby. Legs malformed and crooked, cow-hocked, too long or too short. Stifles straight, coupled with weak hindquarters. Tail unduly short, too low set. Harsh, curly or stand off coat.

Note Male animals should have two apparently normal testicles fully descended into the scrotum.

SUSSEX SPANIEL

General Appearance Massive and strongly built. An active, energetic strong dog, whose characteristic movement is a decided roll, and unlike that of any other Spaniel.

Head and Skull The skull should be wide and show a moderate curve from ear to ear, neither flat nor apple headed, with a centre indentation and a pronounced stop. Brows frowning – occiput decided, but not pointed. Nostrils well developed and liver colour. A well balanced head.

Eyes Hazel colour, fairly large, not too full, but soft expression and not showing the haw over much.

Ears Thick, fairly large and lobe shape, set moderately low but above eye level. Should lie closely, hair soft and wavy, but not too profuse.

Mouth Strong and level, neither over- nor undershot, with a scissor bite.

Neck Long, strong and slightly arched, not carrying the head much above the level of the back. Not much throatiness, but well marked frill.

Forequarters The shoulders should be sloping and free; arms well boned as well as muscular. Knees large and strong, pasterns short and well boned. Legs rather short and strong, moderately well feathered.

Body Chest deep and well developed; not too round and wide. Back and loin well developed and muscular both in width and depth. The back ribs must be deep. Whole body should be strong and level with no sign of waistiness from aitches to hips.

Hindquarters The thighs must be strongly boned as well as muscular; hocks large and strong, legs rather short and strong with good bone, moderately well feathered. The hind legs should not appear shorter than the forelegs, or be too much bent at the hocks so as to give a settery appearance, which is objectionable. The hind legs should be well feathered above the hocks, but not much hair below the hocks.

Feet Circular, well padded, well feathered between toes.

Tail Set low and not carried above level of the back. Free actioned, thickly clothed with hair, but no feather. Docked from 12–18cm (5–7 inches).

Coat Abundant and flat with no tendency to curl and ample under coat for weather resistance.

Colour Rich golden liver and hair shading to gold at the tips: the gold predominating. Not dark liver or puce.

Weight and Size Ideal weight: Dogs 20.4 kilograms (45 pounds); bitches 18.2 kilograms (40 pounds). Height 38–41cm (15–16 inches).

Note Male animals should have two apparently normal testicles fully descended into the scrotum.

141

TIBETAN SPANIEL

Characteristics Gay and assertive, highly intelligent, aloof with strangers.

General Appearance Should be small, active and alert. The outline should give a well-balanced appearance, slightly longer in body than height at withers.

Head and Skull Small in proportion to body and proudly carried, giving an impression of quality. Masculine in dogs but free from coarseness. Skull slightly domed, moderate width and length. Stop slight, but defined. Medium length of muzzle, blunt with cushioning, free from wrinkle. The chin should show some depth and width. Nose: Black preferred.

Eyes Dark brown in colour, oval in shape, bright and expressive, of medium size set fairly well apart but forward looking giving an ape-like expression. Eye rims black.

Ears Medium size, pendant, well feathered in the adult and set fairly high. They may have a slight lift from the skull, but should not fly. Large heavy low set ears are not typical.

Mouth Ideally slightly undershot, the upper incisors fitting neatly inside and touching the lower incisors. Teeth should be evenly placed and the lower jaw wide between the canine tusks. Full dentition desired. A level mouth is permissible providing there is sufficient width and depth of chin to preserve the blunt appearance of muzzle. Teeth must not show when mouth is closed.

Neck Moderately short, strong and well set on. Covered with a mane or 'shawl' of longer hair which is more pronounced in dogs than bitches.

Forequarters The bones of the forelegs slightly bowed but firm at shoulder. Moderate bone. Shoulder well placed.

Body Slightly longer from point of shoulder to root of tail than the height at withers, well ribbed with good depth, level back.

Hindquarters Well made and strong, hocks well let down and straight when viewed from behind. Stifle well developed, showing moderate angulation.

Feet Harefooted, small and neat with feathering between toes often extending beyond the feet. White markings allowed.

Gait Quick moving, straight, free, positive.

Tail Set high, richly plumed and carried in a gay curl over the back when moving. Should not be penalised for dropping tail when standing.

Coat Double coat, silky in texture, smooth on face and front of legs, of moderate length on body, but lying rather flat. Ears and back of forelegs nicely feathered, tail and buttocks well furnished with longer hair. Should not be overcoated and bitches tend to carry less coat and mane than dogs.

Colour All colours and mixture of colours allowed.

Weight and Size 4.1–6.8 kilograms (9–15 pounds) being ideal. Height about 25.4cm (10 inches).

Faults Large full eyes, broad flat muzzle, very domed or flat wide skull, accentuated stop, pointed weak or wrinkled muzzle, overshot mouth, long plain down face without stop, very bowed or loose front, straight stifle, cow hocks, nervousness, cat feet, coarseness of type, mean expression, liver or putty coloured pigmentation, light eyes, protruding tongue.

Note Male animals should have two apparently normal testicles fully descended into the scrotum.

WELSH SPRINGER SPANIEL

Characteristics The 'Welsh Spaniel' or 'Springer' is also known and referred to in Wales as a 'Starter'. He is of very ancient and pure origin, and is a distinct variety.

General Appearance A symmetrical, compact, strong, merry, very active dog; not stilty; obviously built for endurance and hard work. A quick and active mover displaying plenty of push and drive.

Head and Skull Skull proportionate, of moderate length, slightly domed, with clearly defined stop and well chiselled below the eyes. Muzzle of medium length, straight, fairly square; the nostrils well developed and flesh-coloured or dark. A short chubby head is objectionable.

Eyes Hazel or dark, medium size, not prominent, nor sunken, nor showing haw.

Ears Set moderately low and hanging close to the cheeks,

143

comparatively small and gradually narrowing towards the tip and shaped somewhat like a vine leaf, covered with setter-like feathering.

Mouth The jaws should be strong, with a perfect regular and complete scissor bite, ie, the upper teeth closely overlapping the lower teeth and set square to the jaws.

Neck Long and muscular, clean in throat, neatly set into long, sloping shoulders.

Forequarters Forelegs of medium length, straight, well boned, moderately feathered.

Body Not long; strong and muscular with deep brisket, well-sprung ribs; length of body should be proportionate to length of leg, and very well balanced; muscular loin slightly arched and well coupled up.

Hindquarters Strong and muscular, wide and fully developed with deep second thighs. Hind legs well boned, hocks well let down; stifles moderately bent (neither turned in nor out), moderately feathered.

Feet Round, with thick pads. Firm and cat-like, not too large or spreading.

Tail Well set on and low, never carried above the level of the back; lightly feathered and lively in action.

Coat Straight or flat, of a nice silky texture, never wiry nor wavy. A curly coat is most objectionable.

Colour Rich red and white only.

Weight and Size A dog not to exceed 48cm (19 inches) in height at shoulder and a bitch 46cm (18 inches) approximately.

Faults Any departure from the foregoing points should be considered a fault and the seriousness of the fault should be in exact proportion to its degree.

Note Male animals should have two apparently normal testicles fully descended into the scrotum.

10

The Working Spaniel

The working spaniel has long been applauded — indeed as we have seen the spaniel was bred originally as a working dog. It was a fine companion too for the hunter: in days gone by, many country breadwinners were also hunters, and spaniels were also used by both gentry and landowners. 'Sportsmanship' has been in fashion for centuries and a good sporting dog, locating, flushing or springing game and retrieving it after the hunter has shot it, has been worth much money.

Various attributes are needed in a good working dog, including intelligence, a willing disposition, loyalty and an overall desire to please. Stamina is also of prime importance, since the dog is often required to cover a lot of rough ground during a day's shooting, and to retrieve from fast-flowing rivers and dense thickets. The fine qualities of the spaniel are well used. Some working spaniels unfortunately do not have a long life (it could be argued that they do enjoy their shorter one), since they may burn themselves out when working regularly. They will retrieve many scores of birds in a day's shooting, for example, over an area of around 15 miles. Sometimes as many as 1,500 birds are shot in one day – a heavy load for a team of dogs. But they love the work and keep very fit when young.

Smaller strains can make the best working dogs – though this of course is not true of every breed of spaniel. If you intend to work your spaniels, keep that in mind when buying a puppy. Working dogs are best when bred from working parents; they are more easily trained to cope with a working life. Some breeds, such as the Brittany Spaniel, are used almost exclusively for working and make ideal companions only for people who lead a sporting country life. Others of course are better just as companions, needing a softer life.

Not surprisingly there are many fewer working spaniels around than say a hundred years ago. Today the cost of shooting and hunting has escalated. Shooting rights are big

145

Two working English Springer Spaniels sit waiting for the command during a day's pheasant shooting

money. The cost of rearing game birds has risen, and land to shoot over is scarcer. It usually costs something like five times the selling price of a pheasant or partridge to rear one for the gun, and as several thousand birds may be released for shooting in one short season, the total cost is obviously high. At the turn of the century, the average cost per head of game killed was about 3s (15p) and a hand-reared pheasant was costing about 7s (35p) to be 'brought to the gun'. Nowadays that cost is over £10. Furthermore there are fewer professional gamekeepers now, and many amateurs.

Training a Working Spaniel

A sound training is essential for a gundog. It must learn to scent and hunt, point (where possible), flush to a command, drop to shot and retrieve. Obedience is vital, if for no other reason than a dog risks its life in the field if it does not immediately stop when commanded. So having trained a spaniel puppy selected from gundog stock in the basics of obedience, if you want it to go on to be a working companion you start on a course of field training.

As in any other form of training, the foundation is obedience. Having conquered the basics of obedience training, the spaniel subsequently has to learn to 'hunt up', remain still at unshot game, and finally to retrieve efficiently. It should ideally start the field training at the age of about four months, but for a quiet, shy puppy delay it to about six months. It will already be responding to its name and probably to the basic commands, including that of returning on command.

Retrieving can be taught quite simply by throwing an object and commanding the dog to 'fetch'. A soft object such as a glove is best, to help preserve the 'soft-mouth approach' to retrieving which is essential for working spaniels. Extra patience may be needed at this stage to make the puppy drop the object at your feet. During this part of the training exercise, remember not to go towards the dog in an attempt to take the object: the dog will merely run off with it, much appreciating a new game. Most spaniels naturally retrieve – running after a thrown object; the hard part is to get them to bring it straight back, and the most difficult of all is to make them drop it on command.

If the puppy needs encouragement to retrieve, throw the object and, calling him to accompany you, go after it yourself until the dog picks it up. Then take the object from its mouth as you return. It will soon understand the idea. Remember to praise the dog as it learns, and a few minutes at a time is enough.

If the puppy has already been taught to 'sit', the start of the next stage has been accomplished. Then the puppy must learn to remain seated on its haunches while the owner moves off. If, after the command 'wait', it moves off, it must be gently but firmly returned to the exact spot and the exercise repeated until there is reason for praise. When this stage is accomplished the two exercises can be combined to make the spaniel drop down (first) and retrieve a thrown object (second) on command from the dropped (or seated) position.

Returning from the shoot, with successfully retrieved game birds

Next, the puppy must become used to gunfire. This is best achieved by asking someone to fire a gun some distance away when the puppy is feeding and you are close by. The puppy will be too busy with its food to be alarmed. Gradually, as the training sessions progress, the gun should be fired progressively closer to the dog and the command given to drop. In time the puppy will associate the gunfire with the command to drop and will do so *when the shot is fired*. This is necessary for a successful gundog.

When a spaniel puppy reaches about six months old it will begin to discover its keen ability to scent and will start to use this talent to advantage. It is then that a gundog in training will learn to distinguish the different field scents and to curb its natural enthusiasm to investigate them with much activity. The merry spaniel much enjoys making use of its sense of smell to trail a rabbit or squirrel. A gundog, however, must be taught to distinguish but not to chase. A rabbit in a pen will be a good aid to this lesson, and it will quickly learn not to chase. Later, in the field, the dog will be able to scent and 'put up' a rabbit and drop immediately so that the game can be shot. Having trained the gundog thus far, refinement is necessary and much practice to make perfect. The use of freshly shot game in the field will help the dog to become familiar with the idea of its work.

The final refinement is to teach the dog the systems of 'quartering'. A good gundog will work systematically from side to side covering as much ground as possible searching for game. It will work best within a radius of about twenty-five yards of its owner, who will probably use whistled commands rather than voiced ones in order to disturb any game as little as possible before the dog has found it.

A good, well-trained working gundog is as much a joy to watch as a good sheepdog. The dog will enjoy its part in the team and respond well in its work, keeping its interest in the natural world around it.

Some spaniels, such as the Springer and Cocker, are often used by the beaters to spring or flush game. On a shoot where many people are participating, other dogs may be used to retrieve the fallen birds after they have been shot. But the spaniel which works alone with its owner has to find, flush and retrieve game, and most working spaniels will be trained for all these tasks. Others may be worked by being trained 'for the gun' in basic terms and taught to retrieve for owners who simply shoot rabbits or pigeons, for example, on their own land or on large estates or farms with the landlord's permission.

Spaniels in these situations are ideal companions and are trained easily to retrieve from thick coverts, water or open land with equal success, depending on the breed used. The Irish Water Spaniel, for example, was much recommended early in the century for its recognisable talents in finding snipe; it was trained to point and retrieve. Today it remains a popular dog for wildfowlers, as its aquatic retrieving habits are outstanding. Its curly coat, however, hampers it a little in undergrowth, while the silkier coat of a Cocker is ideal here.

Today pheasant, partridge and grouse are the game birds most usually shot with the help of dogs, including spaniels. Pheasants, for example, are usually retrieved from coverts and driven downhill to the waiting guns. Partridges are generally driven into a root field where they can more easily be retrieved. The partridge is a more difficult bird to shoot, too, because unlike grouse or pheasant which 'rocket' towards the marksmen, it twists and swerves in the air.

Snipe behave in the same way, but there are not many of these around these days. Grouse can be found north of the River Trent, in Shropshire, Wales, Scotland and Ireland, and spaniels are particularly popular for retrieving them – and as beaters' dogs, driving the game towards the guns in a line of 'butts'. Quick retrieving is important since there is only a short time available for picking up the dead birds, so spaniels with speed and stamina are needed. The method of driving grouse down towards the line of guns was started around 1805 and spaniels were used not only for the driving and retrieving but also as 'flankers' dogs', working continuously on the flanks of the driving teams to turn the birds inwards to the guns before they took to the air. In grouse shooting, as in other shoots, care should be taken to work your spaniel up-wind if possible, and in warm, calm weather to beat the higher ground thoroughly for the birds. In stormy weather grouse seek the lower slopes.

Two centuries ago when we had lost so much less land to roads, industry and housing, it would have been pleasant to potter off with one's spaniels into the local woodland to 'bag' a pheasant or a rabbit for the pot. This is still possible in some country areas, but in Britain, at least, this is becoming difficult for most of us. It must be the best way to work a spaniel – rather than the 'factory' method of slaughtering scores or hundreds of birds which, while a good 'sporting' event for some, for many of us lacks appeal.

11

Emergencies and First Aid

If your spaniel is injured or unwell, you have quickly to decide whether or not you need the help of a veterinary surgeon. Quite often, instinct in an emergency situation helps you take the right action, or near-enough the right action. An incident with one of my Springers illustrates this. We were walking in woodland when he gave me a distinct warning that 'something' was hidden in a thicket. He stood still, just his tail wagging furiously, in front of the brambles, and when I peered in I saw what appeared in the gloom to be a fawn, a young deer, injured in some way. Deciding to see if I could help the animal, I foolishly told the dog to 'stay' and went round the other side of the thicket to try to get through to it.

I heard, rather than saw, the result of my lack of thought. The injured animal was no fawn but an adult muntjac stag with both its front legs broken – probably having been hit by a car, or perhaps having an accident when jumping a fence. It was lucky for my dog that the poor deer's legs were broken, since at least that slowed down his charge. Muntjacs have razor-sharp horns. As my spaniel stood his ground the deer crashed into his shoulder, slicing the shoulder muscle as it did so.

This all happened in a few seconds. I heard the crash and howl of pain from the dog, rushed back to the front of the thicket and saw the deer kneeling in front of the spaniel, which had been completely bowled over. Instinct was the only resource I had, and picking up the dog I held him close to my chest to staunch the flow of blood from his wound. I ran to the car, bundled us both in, and with the dog still against my chest drove to the vet. The wound needed sixteen stitches but healed quite quickly, leaving little scarring and only a slightly stiff shoulder in old age.

The humorous side to the incident came when I left the vet, who was stitching up the dog under anaesthetic, to go and telephone the local gamekeeper about destroying the injured deer. I forgot the state of my shirtfront, and must have looked a terrible sight as I came out. A passer-by frightened me and those about her by screaming 'Oh my God, he's been shot! Help, someone, help!' Several people rushed to my aid and I had to explain what had happend before they would let me get into the car!

If I had handled this incident 'by the book', various things would have been done better. I would have looked more closely at the injured deer before stationing the dog near it. Muntjac deer, and many other medium-sized mammals such as roe deer, badgers, foxes, etc, can be dangerous when wounded. Then, when the dog was injured, I was right to staunch the blood flow, but a better way would have been to tear up a clean part of my clothing and bind the shoulder in a makeshift way, keeping the edges of the wound together and holding a pad in place with strips. However, the job was done adequately, though the safety-minded amongst us would have had something to say about people driving at top speed with a spaniel across their laps.

Wounds

Gaping wounds need stitching and professional treatment from a vet. Foot wounds, for example, are usually a trouble, because they so easily become infected; antibiotics may be needed.

Smaller wounds can often be treated quite simply. Any wound should be cleansed. Wash your hands and then gently cut away any surrounding fur, making sure no cut hairs fall into the wound. (Temporarily cover the wound with a clean piece of soft lint gauze soaked in warm water while the cutting is being done.) Do not put iodine or any other disinfectant into the wound, but examine its progress twice a day. If it is pink and clean, all is well. If there is a discharge from it, this must be gently bathed away with boiled warm water. A wound should heal from inside and if a scab forms it may hold any pus forming underneath, aggravating the infection.

Watch a wounded spaniel carefully, looking out for symptoms that may indicate an infection, such as lack of appetite, listlessness, obvious pain. You know the dog and

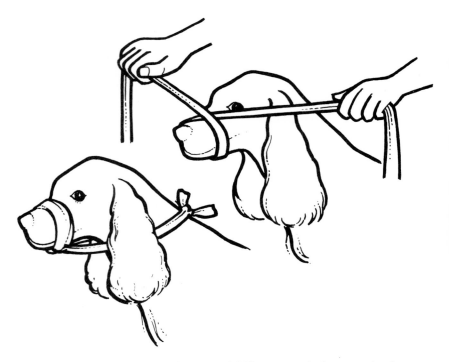

Two simple steps in muzzling a spaniel if necessary before examination or treatment of a painful wound

you should be able to tell if complications appear. That is the time for advice from the vet.

Dog fights often lead to wounds and possibly infection. If your dog has been in a fight, examine it carefully for bites. Small bites can be as serious as large ones. Cleanse them with warm water and treat them as for other wounds. Often a bitten spaniel will go into shock after the harrowing experience of a fight, and this could well indicate an infection – look for sub-normal temperature, pale gums and the sort of lethargy and loss of appetite mentioned above.

Chest, throat or abdominal wounds – often caused when the dog jumps railings or barbed-wire fences, by dog fights or attacks from other animals, or even a fall from a height – should be taken extremely seriously. In the case of an abdominal gash, a warm saline-soaked bandage should be wound round the dog's body as a support for the abdomninal wall, and treatment by a veterinary surgeon sought immediately. Throat and chest wounds too should be seen by a vet as quickly as possible.

If bitten by an adder (unlikely, but a dog occasionally disturbs one sunning itself), a swelling may appear at the site of the bite, and the dog may become listless. A vet will inject an antiserum, as a doctor would for humans.

A device known as the 'Elizabethan collar' can be a useful aid to healing a wound or skin disorder which is being 'worried' by the dog. Simply cut a circular piece of stiff cardboard or plastic about 45cm (18in) in diameter. Then cut a circular hole of a size that will fit over the dog's head so the collar will rest comfortably on its neck. A V-shaped piece should then be cut out, with the point of the V at the central hole. Small holes are punched, or dug with scissor-points, on either side of the V. Insert laces, and when the collar is around the dog's neck, lace up hole to hole. When in place it resembles a shallow saucer, and it stops the dog licking, scratching or chewing itself anywhere behind the collar. If unsteady it can be clipped to the dog's own collar.

Making and fitting an 'Elizabethan collar'

155

Broken Limbs

Broken limbs should be held immobile by a rigid splint bound round with fabric, until the dog reaches the vet. If any other bones are broken, such as pelvis, ribs, shoulder or, especially, the back, the dog should remain still until the vet arrives.

Burns and Scalds

Burns and scalds are a source of trouble to dogs and can often be avoided with a little care in the home. It is a spaniel's nature to follow its owner around and this trait is especially evident when food is about. If you are cooking, try to keep the dog away from the cooker and from under your feet. Quite apart from the obvious dangers resulting from tripping over the dog yourself, there is the danger of hot water, fat or other liquid dripping onto the dog's coat. The result of this will not be immediately evident since the dog's coat will absorb and intensify the scalding, so treatment should be rapid. If the dog is scalded, get the affected area quickly under cold, slowly running water. This minimises the shock which almost certainly accompanies either scalding or burning. If the area affected is small, a coating of Acriflex or Savlon ointment should be applied to it. The dog will certainly require veterinary treatment since the risks of both shock and infection are substantial, and in any case burns and scalds are extremely painful, and pain-relievers will be needed.

Burns, caused by a dry heat as opposed to the wet heat of scalding, require veterinary attention quickly for the same reasons. For burns, a pad of gauze or lint soaked in bicarbonate of soda (25g [1oz] to ½ litre [1pt] of boiled and cooled water) is one form of treatment, but this takes time to prepare and the dog is suffering; so treatment as for scalding will save time. Bicarbonate of soda can also be used in the case of chemical or acid burning.

Prevention is much better than cure – always observe simple precautions, such as keeping dogs away from an active cooker, putting household chemicals well out of reach, and keeping dogs well away from bonfires, fireworks (which are always a curse if animals are around), boiling kettles and other potential sources of danger.

156

If you wish to keep your spaniel out of the way while you are cooking or dishing-up hot food, but would still like it to be with you, try a system which has been most useful in my own household. I have a metal 'gate' of the sort used to prevent babies from climbing or falling down stairs. The gate is adjustable in width by means of a movable rubber block at the end of each of two arms. If your kitchen, like mine, has no door separating it from the rest of the house, or you like to keep the door open, the gate can be fitted between the door jambs with the spaniel on the far side. They can see what is going on without getting under your feet. This gate is also useful for confining dogs to a particular area – for example when they are drying off after a bath or wet walk.

Electric Shocks and Burns

An obvious and often overlooked source of danger is the electric flex. Electric shocks *may* not kill a puppy, but the chances are heavily in favour of death if it chews through the cable of a lamp or any other household appliance. Puppies love chewing and are often attracted by a snakelike electric lead, playing with it and then chewing it through; if it is connected, you stand a grave risk of losing your puppy. If it is lucky enough not to be killed it will probably lose consciousness and receive burns to the mouth. *Turn off the current.* Then, if the dog has stopped breathing, try artificial respiration – placing the dog on its side and alternately pressing down on and releasing the ribcage, at intervals of two or three seconds.

Drowning

Similar treatment (see above) can be given to a drowned dog, although in this case the dog should first be held head-down and swung back and forth several times.

Heat Exhaustion

Another accident to dogs that should never happen. No dog can be left for any length of time in a car in the sun – and so many drivers forget this basic piece of commonsense! The inside of a car, even if two windows are partially opened, can rapidly heat up on a sunny day to temperatures well over 32°C

157

(90°F). A dog will become extremely distressed and will subsequently lose consciousness due to hyperthermia. Since a dog does not sweat but relies on panting to lose excess heat, it can succumb to heat exhaustion very quickly. It may collapse or have convulsions, and if not treated promptly it will die.

Treatment consists of removing the dog to a shady place and dowsing the head, neck and upper part of the body with cold water, until it revives. Allowing a dog to get into this state is inexcusable.

Choking

This is one of the most alarming accidents to dogs. All possible preventative measures should always be taken. Keep small swallowable playthings away from a dog – particularly while it is a puppy. A common cause of choking, which few owners appear to recognise, are small balls, such as children's toys, rubber squash balls or golf balls. Puppies often play with such things while rolling on their backs, holding them lightly in their jaws: in this position a small ball can slip into the throat and become lodged. Make sure that no ball smaller than a tennis ball is given to a spaniel.

If a dog does get some object wedged in its throat, it will die of asphyxiation within minutes if not aided. Desperate measures are needed. Insert a finger quickly into the dog's throat and try to hook out the object blocking the air passage. If this proves impossible, the only other thing is to push the object down. If two people are around this will help, as one can hold the jaws open while the other attends to the object. Either or both may be bitten during the process, as the dog will be terrified.

This frightening description shows how necessary it is to pay close attention to the things a dog or puppy is playing with, and to remove at once anything small enough to get stuck in the throat. Even the dog's food needs care – it must be given in small pieces, since most spaniels normally bolt their food, and large chunks of meat or anything else could cause choking.

Poisoning

Veterinary treatment is needed immediately in most

poisoning cases, but if you know what it is that has poisoned your dog you can begin the treatment by giving an antidote while the vet is awaited.

In *any* case of poisoning – even if you are unsure whether the dog did actually swallow it – be safe rather than sorry and give the dog an emetic, such as ordinary salt in 150ml (¼pt) water. After the dog has vomited, and while waiting for the vet, you can give egg-whites beaten in milk. If you know exactly what the poison is, and if it is one of those noted below, you can treat as suggested while you wait.

The antidotes for *arsenic* are Epsom salts, barley water or diluted olive oil. Also give egg-whites beaten in milk.

If the dog has swallowed *acids*, give bicarbonate of soda. If it has consumed one of the usual *household cleaning agents*, which are alkaline, give vinegar or lemon juice.

Iodine poisoning should be treated with arrowroot or cornflour with Kaolin and morphine.

For *strychnine* poisoning, give butter, dripping or other fats; for this, an injection of Apomorphia by the vet will be essential very quickly, and after the immediate emetic and subsequent butter treatment, keep the dog quiet in a darkened room.

Mercury is contained in rat poisons and some human skin ointments, and while egg whites will help, immediate veterinary treatment is needed.

Match tips contain *phosphorous* (which is also common in rodent poisons). If a dog or puppy has chewed these, give Epsom salts after the emetic while you await the vet.

Lead poisoning is possible after licking paints, and egg-whites, after the emetic has worked, are a good antidote, beaten in milk and added to a little Milk of Magnesia solution. About a dessert spoonful of Epsom salts in 150ml (¼pt) warm water, following irrigation of the stomach with salt water, is useful treatment.

These notes are guidelines for immediate treatment, but get the vet just as soon as you can when a dog is poisoned. Describe the symptoms to him when you call him, and tell him what the poison is if you can.

The poisoning of dogs should, though, be prevented rather than cured. Keep household substances away from them. The use of garden weedkillers, insecticides, slug baits, rat poisons, etc, must be risky when dogs are around.

The Spaniel's First-Aid Box

When putting a first-aid box together for your spaniel – see list below; this is a sensible precaution against accidents and general disorders – include eucalyptus oil, but not only because of its use in the removal of ticks. It is also an effective solvent for the removal of tar and motor oil from dogs' feet. Anyone whose spaniel runs on a beach or 'helps' in the garage will know how difficult this job can be. Whether the tar appears on the coat or on the feet, soak a swab of cotton wool or gauze with eucalyptus oil and rub it well into the affected part. Dry cottonwool or gauze can then be used to wipe it all off together. The dog's feet or coat can then be washed in warm soapy water (or bathed in a dog shampoo if the coverage is extensive) and dried off.

You may also care to include a few of the more common herbal remedies. They are quite safe to use and can be obtained from most good herbalists, providing useful additions to a dog's general care. Garlic, for example, is a good internal purifier, strong in vitamins A, B1 and C, and in calcium, phosphorous and iron. It can be useful in the prevention of worms and other casually acquired ailments.

Rhubarb *in herbal form* – not its raw state – can be a useful laxative, and seaweed-powder preparations are a good tonic and coat toner. Charcoal is quite effective against bad breath and indigestion, helping to tone up the digestive system.

There is a preparation known as 'leaf plasma' (available in Britain from Herb Royal of Bridgwater, Somerset) which is said to contain a mixture of nettles, grasses, liquorice and magnesium and to be a good nerve tonic, also increasing vitality. Skullcap (the plant *Scutellaria*, often called helmet flower because it resembles the helmet of a Roman soldier) is also considered to be a good nerve tonic for spaniels. Herbal preparations of this kind often include peony root, vervain and rosemary – all held to have nerve-soothing properties.

A supply of rock sulphur, obtainable from pet stores or chemist, and added to the dog's drinking-bowl, is a blood-purifier and general conditioner.

160

Honey should also be on hand, though you may prefer to keep it in your food cupboard rather than the dog's first-aid box! it is useful to help ease stomach upsets and light fever; give it in water when a dog cannot keep down solid food, and in cases of diarrhoea and vomiting.

The first-aid box should also include a bottle of TCP, which is a useful antiseptic (use one part in five parts of water) and especially valuable in relieving wasp or bee stings. Disprins make mild pain-relievers – give a half to one tablet in water, every four hours.

A good supply of absorbent lint, gauze, cotton-wool and dressings must be kept scrupulously clean, ready for use. Add steel forceps with rounded tips, and a pair of sharp scissors, also with rounded tips, to cut dressing material and the hair from around a wound. If sterilisation is needed, eg when dressing a wound, remember to boil the scissors used to cut the dressing at the same time.

A blunt-ended clinical thermometer should also be in the box, and a tube of Vaseline to lubricate it (more hygienic than a jar).

SPANIEL'S FIRST-AID AND MEDICINE BOX

Round-tipped scissors
Round-ended plastic forceps
Clinical thermometer
Glass medicine-dropper and rubber teat
2 plastic syringes (20ml)
Bandages
Gauze pads
Cottonwool balls
Absorbent lint
Double-sided surgical tape
Clean towelling
Dish (stainless steel)

Vaseline (tube)
Savlon or Acriflex (tube)
Bob Martin's 92 antiseptic ointment (tube)
TCP (bottle)
Eucalyptus oil (bottle)

Dog shampoo (eg Phillips Yeast Products, Sherley's, etc)
Sherley's 'Dogband' or Canovel flea collar
Alugan sachets (Hoechst), for flea and lice treatment
Insecticidal dog powder (puffer)
Zemol powder (Phillips Yeast Products) for skin troubles
Amplex veterinary deodorant tablets (Ashe Labs) for in-season bitches
Worming tablets, eg Beecham's Canovel
Powdered alum
Epsom salts
Bicarbonate of soda
Disprins
Milk of Magnesia (bottle)
Salt
Kaobiotic tablets
Kaolin and morphine (bottle)
Miniature brandy
Pure olive oil
Pure cod-liver oil
Rock sulphur (eg Sherley's)
Glucose
Honey

12

Medical Care, Disorders and Illnesses

A nineteenth-century breeder of spaniels who commented that a dog's owner is better placed to know when something is wrong with it than a veterinary surgeon was entirely right. The same breeder pointed out that having concluded that the dog is ill, you must then ascertain whether or not it is in pain, examining it all over carefully for tenderness, swelling, excessive heat, or a dry, staring coat. Very cold ears, very hot thighs, a dry, brown or coated tongue, a bloodshot or yellow eye, a scurvy skin, bad breath, continued quick breathing or wheezing – all of these may indicate a sick dog. Add such symptoms as vomiting and/or diarrhoea, and there is certainly something amiss which requires treatment. If the temperature is high (or very low) in addition – and taking a spaniel's temperature is described on page 167 – the remedy is needed with some speed.

A dog you know will also tell you by its expression if it is unwell – a pinched, nervous expression, or one of fear or discomfort, which only you may recognise, are warning signs. Be aware of your dog and by its actions and expressions you will know its state of health.

This book cannot deal with every disease a spaniel could have: there are as many as for any other dog or for a human being. If you feel that the dog is sick – and if you have a close association with it you will know – and if you have tried the basic remedies for the less serious conditions without effect, then the dog must see a veterinary surgeon. If you are ever in any doubt about the dog's health and about what to do, then seek this advice.

A dog should if possible be visited in its own home by the vet, after you have telephoned the surgery with details of the symptoms. This is less distressing for the dog than having to sit in a crowded surgery waiting-room with a multitude of sick or boisterous animals. A dog which has paid one or two visits to a surgery will make itself worse with fear when it goes there again. This will not affect its state of health if it is there simply to receive an injection or be examined for a minor ailment such as a skin irritation, for example, but it will do it harm if it is really ill.

In some urban areas vets discourage requests for home visits and insist on their patients attending surgery unless in an extreme emergency; and indeed a vet like a doctor may be heavily laden with work. Quite often, too, much of the equipment a vet needs for a thorough examination will be in the surgery. The dog-owner, however, unlike a country doctor's patient, can usually choose where to go. If your dog is sick and you feel that sitting in a surgery waiting-room will increase its distress, then say so. If the vet, or his receptionist, still insists that you bring the dog to the surgery, seek around, if there is time, till you find a vet who will visit you. Having arranged a visit, then do not complain when you find that the bill is more than for a surgery visit – it is worth it for the patient.

Diseases or disorders often need the services of a vet, but it is up to the owner to evaluate whether or not symptoms are dangerous. It is your responsibility to see that your dog is kept fit and well whenever possible and that its welfare is always carefully considered. Even minor disorders need treatment – such as constipation, which, while not always serious in itself, still causes discomfort to the dog. Such disorders should usually be prevented – in this case by suitable food and exercise – but if they occur you should be aware of them right away and treat them promptly.

Giving Medicine
Sometimes you are lucky enough to be able to give the dog a powder crushed into its food, or to have it accepted from your hand, but usually a special technique is needed. Your spaniel will probably be just the same as others when it comes to taking medicine: it will close its mouth firmly and look at you with a hurt expression that tears at the heartstrings. Nonetheless the medicine must be swallowed and it is best to get on with the job in a firm but gentle way.

164

Holding a spaniel ready to give medicine or tablets

Giving medicine with a syringe inserted between the teeth and directed towards the throat

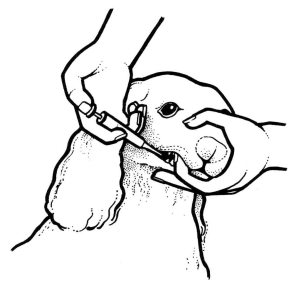

If a tablet has to be taken in solid form, hold it between your thumb and forefinger, and with the other hand and the middle finger of the hand holding the tablet, open the dog's mouth. By applying pressure on the palate from the thumb of the free hand, the mouth can be prevented from closing. Place the tablet as far back on the tongue towards the throat as possible, and close the dog's mouth. Holding the head upwards (but not too far back for the dog to swallow), gently massage the throat until the tablet is swallowed.

One of my spaniels learned to twist the tablet deftly to one side just as her mouth was closed and then pretend quite dramatically to swallow it. She would wander around innocently until she thought I was not looking, and then spit it out behind a chair or in some other secluded place. Giving her tablets became a battle of wits, with the accent on speed, but I usually won in the end – sheer practice making perfect!

Liquid medicines are easier to give, and I find the best way of giving them – and of giving tablets if they can be crushed into a powder and suspended in warm water – is with the aid of a 20ml plastic syringe. These can be bought from a chemist or medical supplies firm, and although disposable can be used several times if cleaned out thoroughly each time. The technique is simple because the dog's mouth can remain closed throughout.

Dilute the crushed tablet or powder in warm water in a small glass or beaker, or pour the dose of a liquid medicine straight into the receptacle. Fill the syringe from it. Take hold of the spaniel's muzzle firmly in one hand, and with the thumb at the back of the lips, gently lift the lips apart to expose the back teeth. Keeping the dog's muzzle closed and tilted upwards, insert the syringe nozzle between the teeth and gently but steadily expel the liquid in the direction of the throat, allowing time for the dog to swallow in between. If there is more than one syringeful to be given, refill the syringe with one hand and repeat the procedure. Do not use a metal syringe as this is uncomfortable for the dog and will antagonise it: and obviously a glass one would break.

Alternatively, if giving liquid medicine without a syringe, hold the spaniel close to your body, preferably on a non-slippery table, with your hand on its chest. Take hold of its muzzle with the other hand, parting the lips with your fingers. If the dog is in a comfortable position, with its head against your chest, you can pour in the medicine between the parted lips, towards the back of the mouth, slowly so that the dog does not choke; then again, hold up the head and gently massage the throat. If giving powders, this method can be used with the help of an assistant, who can pour the powder through the dog's lips from a paper funnel.

Taking a Dog's Temperature

Lubricate a clinical thermometer with Vaseline, and gently insert it into the dog's rectum. Hold the dog still for a full minute – if it moves around the thermometer could be broken and the dog badly injured. Then withdraw and read the thermometer, shake it down and disinfect it.

A dog's normal temperature is 38.6°C (101.5°F), and young puppies often have a normal temperature of up to 39°C (102°F). If a spaniel's temperature is over 39.2°C (102.5°F) it is abnormally high and should it reach 39.5C (103°F) it is seriously high. A dog may be equally ill if its temperature is subnormal, below 37.8°C (100°F), except that a bitch about to deliver her puppies may quite normally have a temperature as low as 37.2°C (99°F).

Taking a Dog's Pulse

Place a finger on the artery which crosses the femur, the longest bone of the upper leg, inside the thigh. There should be between 70 and 90 beats a minute. The rate is faster in a small dog, slower in a large one, with an average of 85 beats in a healthy medium-size dog such as a Cocker Spaniel. A high pulse rate can indicate illness or infection, and a slow rate is found in heart failure or pneumonia.

Pulse rates and temperature readings, coupled with your observations of the spaniel's overall condition, movements and reactions, can be combined with any other symptoms to make a diagnosis. If considered serious the vet should be called upon for advice.

Ear Troubles

Some people always expect a spaniel to have ear troubles and

167

a substantial problem is indeed caused by grass seeds. In the summer, particularly around July, it may be advisable to seek exercise areas where there is not much long, seeding grass. Some seeds, especially the tor or more ferocious couch or 'arrow' types of grass seeds, get caught in the fur of the ear flap and then work their way down inside the ear. If not removed, they can get deep down inside causing much pain and distress, and can even eventually cause death. If a seed is present, the spaniel will be in obvious distress, shaking its head back and forth and crying out. Never poke instruments into the ear, but drop a little warm olive oil into it, which may help relieve the immediate irritation. Clean the inside of the flap gently with soft cottonwool, and if the seed is near the edge you may be able to remove it in this way. If a sharp seed is well down in the ear, however, the dog must see a vet so that it can be professionally removed – often this is done under anaesthetic.

Grass seeds can also be a source of infection in a dog's feet, but from there they can usually be safely removed. If they have become embedded in the soft skin between a spaniel's toes, they should be gently removed from the front of the wound, which is then cleansed with boiled warm water.

The other ear trouble for spaniels is canker, recognisable by a dark brown, sticky mud-like wax, reddening of the inner ear and often a swelling and smelly discharge. It can be dry or wet. Treatment consists of cleaning the accessible part of the ear with soft wedges of cotton-wool and dropping in a suitable remedy such as Otosporin, obtainable from the veterinary surgeon or a chemist. Beware of powder treatments for canker: powders often clog up the ear and further complicate the process of cleaning it out. Use a liquid, in small drops, slightly warmed. The ear should be gently cleaned at least once a day, and if the condition persists the dog should see a vet.

Ear conditions can be dangerous in the long term, since the infection can spread into the brain. Normally a thorough inspection of a spaniel's ears at least once a week will detect early signs of canker, which can then be treated carefully before it becomes chronic. Care in ensuring that the insides of the ears are kept dry also helps. Remember that the ear is delicate and the inside should never be poked about, even with cottonwool wrapped round a stick.

Eye Troubles

Sometimes a spaniel will have a weeping eye. It may be due to various problems, one being conjunctivitis, which could be due to infection or dust or grit in the eye. There is also lower-eyelash irritation on the eyeball, a condition known as 'entropion'. Where the eyelids turn slightly outwards, and consequently fail to provide sufficient protection against dust or grit, the condition is known as 'ectropion'. Eye-weeping can also be due to a blocked tear-duct. Never let a spaniel put its head out of the window of a moving car as this can be very dangerous to the eyes, which take the onslaught of strong winds containing grit and dust; this can lead to conjunctivitis and other eye problems.

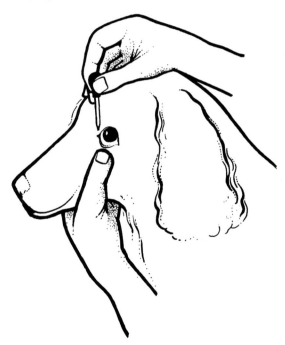

Inserting eye drops

169

Simple eye infections can be treated with a suitable preparation, but a vet's diagnosis is needed if the condition worsens. If irritation is evident, through a speck of grit or a small seed, these can often be flushed out by dropping a warm salt solution into the eye. Again, eyes are extremely sensitive organs, so never use any instrument to poke around the eyelids. A weak solution of alum powder is helpful for bathing a sore eye: dissolve about a level teaspoonful in 400ml (¾pt) warm water, and bathe with soft cottonwool two or three times a day.

Tooth Problems

Spaniels rarely have much in the way of dental problems; certainly cavities are rare. In old age the teeth may need scaling through a build-up of tartar. I have in fact scaled accessible teeth myself, with the aid of the milled edge of a 10p piece pressed against the tooth just below the gum. Normally the tartar flakes off quite easily. Old spaniels may need teeth extracted if they become really bad and painful or if there is a build-up of tartar down into the gum which causes infection. A visit to the vet will sort this out.

Generally, disorders of the teeth can be prevented by a proper diet. Too much soft food with no large bones to gnaw, or dog biscuits to chew, will cause tartar to appear in later life. If the dog's breath is bad or he is salivating a good deal he may have some form of problem in his mouth and should be examined by a vet.

Breast Tumours

Some unspayed female spaniels will develop breast tumours in old age but they are not necessarily malignant. Nonetheless, they will probably need to be surgically removed if they continue to grow, although treatment by the vet with testosterone (hormone injections) sometimes reduces them if attended to early. If you notice any lumps on the underside of your spaniel bitch, take her to the vet immediately.

Arthritis

One of the diseases usually attacking older dogs, rather than younger ones, is arthritis. It affects heavier, fatter dogs far worse than those which are slimmer. Old age tends to bring on a certain stiffness of the joints and extra weight will exacerbate the situation if arthritis is present. Warmth and dry living areas free of draughts, and extra patience when walking so that the dog does not have to struggle to keep up, are both helpful courses of action. Aspirin is the most common treatment, with cortisone or phenylbutazone administered by the vet in extreme cases.

Diabetes

This is another disease which occurs more often in fat dogs than in those of normal weight. Sudden weight loss is a symptom, accompanied by a noticeable thirst and consequently increased urination. It is not the only disease which is accompanied by a strong thirst and, if your spaniel is continuously drinking much more water than usual, it should be watched carefully, since there could be a problem requiring veterinary attention.

Diabetes can also be recognised by vomiting, although this is more likely in severe cases. The less serious cases can be helped by a reduction of carbohydrate in the diet; replace it by boiled fish, chicken breast or eggs. If the disease does not respond, either insulin injections or tablets will be needed regularly, as in a diabetic human. Although a good deal of extra attention to the dog is needed in this way, it can still lead a normal life. Some diabetic dogs live to good ages if careful attention is given to insulin dosage.

Cystitis

Another disease – more usually acute than chronic – which is evidenced by frequent urination is cystitis. It can be diagnosed quite easily since there will be pain in the area of the kidneys and bladder and the spaniel will be very restless. The cause may only be a mild infection which can be cleared up by antibiotics obtained from the vet, or it may be due to a stone. In the latter case there is often blood present in the urine and surgery is usually required.

Fungal Attacks

Attacks by various forms of fungus occur occasionally,

171

producing red bald spots on the skin, which are usually itchy and tender causing much irritation to the dog. The vet will prescribe a suitable antifungal preparation to clear up the problem. Recovery is often speeded during treatment by putting on the 'Elizabethan collar' mentioned earlier.

Respiratory and Heart Conditions

Spaniels, like humans, can have a variety of respiratory disorders. The so-called 'kennel cough' is one of them, and is usually associated with boarding kennels and dog pounds. This harsh, dryish cough is noticed after exercise or when the dog is excited. A cough can of course be a symptom of heart disease or of canine distemper, but prevention of the latter is assisted by the immunisation course given to your spaniel in puppyhood by the vet.

For any respiratory infection, keep the dog warm (and dry in wet weather), give it peace and solitude and bathe away any nasal discharge with warm saline solution. A sick dog needs rest, quiet and reassurance, with minimum disturbance. If the condition worsens, or lasts for some days, seek the help of a vet. Dogs can sometimes pick up influenza, and some are susceptible to hay fever. The latter is usually accompanied by a skin irritation and probably conjunctivitis.

If any bronchial infection worsens there is a danger of broncho-pneumonia, the symptoms including shivering, fever and a high temperature, rapid pulse, laboured breathing and evident distress. Veterinary treatment is essential immediately.

Spaniels are no more prone to heart disease than other breeds (unless they are allowed to get fat), but it is as well to know what to look for so that suitable precautions, exercise and/or medication can be provided. One of the first signs of heart disease is often a short, sharp 'huffing' cough. The heartbeat is often irregular and 'thready' or muffled, as well as slow, and the dog listless, sometimes with falling coat and dull eyes.

The abdomen sometimes becomes distended, and the dog will be slow, and uninterested in moving around, and also lose weight. A heart problem does not necessarily mean that the dog is at the end of its life: some conditions are quite easy to manage, with or without medication. The trouble could be, for example, a mild mitral-valve malfunction or heart murmur which could improve – or at least be controlled – if you are aware of it and do not overtax the dog; it would need a suitable diet, including a good deal of fresh meat and some boiled rice, and some dogs need a regular maintenance dose of tablets prescribed by the vet.

Uterine Problems
Metritis can occur in a bitch as an acute or chronic condition. In the acute form, often caused by retention of a placenta (see Chapter 5, Breeding), there is a high fever, often vomiting and diarrhoea, and a highly toxic discharge from the uterus. This can generally be prevented by ensuring that all placentas and foetuses are clear after a litter has been born. The chronic form of metritis is less evident and is a milder form of inflammation of the uterus; the bitch is often restless and will have only a mild infection. The only remedy really is a total hysterectomy. This is one disease which spaying does prevent.

Pyometra is a similar disorder but one in which there is a dangerous build-up of pus in the uterus, often originating from some mild infection. It is mostly found in bitches which have not had a litter, and can usually be recognised by an intermittent vaginal discharge, although this is not always so. Mild infection is accompanied by a mild fever and the bitch will be listless with a somewhat distended abdomen – rather as if she was pregnant. As in the case of metritis, a total hysterectomy is the only real remedy.

In both situations, the operation is considered more risky when the bitch has toxaemia or a high fever, and the vet may prescribe antibiotics at first to reduce this and even beat the infection. Both conditions, however, are likely to recur unless a hysterectomy is undertaken.

Digestive Upsets and Disorders
Diarrhoea is usually a symptom of some other condition, or an indication that a spaniel's diet is not quite right. Sometimes it occurs during a change of diet. A vet told me that Christmas is a busy time for dogs with upset stomachs; it

173

seems that people like their dogs to overeat as well as themselves, so that they too 'have a good time'. But do not pad the dog's diet with rich Christmas foods because you and your family enjoy them: they will do the poor dog more harm than good. Food it is not used to eating will almost certainly upset its stomach.

A spaniel suffering from diarrhoea can be helped by being starved of solid food for 24 hours, while being given plenty of cool boiled water to drink, and doses of a kaolin mixture. The vet will probably supply a kaolin tablet with an infection-fighting drug in it, called Kaobiotic. A little of the kaolin and morphine mixture that humans use can be equally helpful to a dog, but it should be diluted – about a teaspoonful of the mixture in half a glass of water once or twice a day, for two or three days.

After the first day give a light diet – say of boiled fish or white chicken meat, with natural yoghurt or boiled rice mixed with it – for a few days. If there is no improvement, then get veterinary advice – as should be done at once if the dog is in pain or entirely off its food.

A sick dog with a bad digestive disorder can be maintained on the following mixture, dripped through the back teeth slowly from a syringe and given every hour in dessertspoonfuls: one egg white, one tablespoonful each of boiled water and milk, and a dessertspoonful of glucose or honey, all beaten together. The dog should also have boiled cool water available to drink, with a teaspoonful of salt added to every pint of water. The mixture, given every hour, night and day, plus a lot of care for some four days, helped save the life of that Springer spaniel of mine with haemorrhagic gastro-enteritis, a very dangerous disease. For three days and three nights continually when the vet told me that the chances of recovery were not good, I sat with the dog all the time, soothing the painful abdominal spasms which accompany the disease, dripping the solution into his mouth and every four hours carrying him gently into the garden to relieve himself. He was so weak that he had to be held up each time. I rarely left his side, and on the morning of the third day he moved a little on the couch where he was wrapped. His tail gave a few feeble waves, and I knew that he was on the way to recovery.

If your dog should be seriously ill, its recovery does mainly depend on three factors: expert veterinary treatment, good nursing accompanied by quiet surroundings and soothing attention, and last but not least the will to get better. I believe it is worth giving up everything for a few days to nurse a very sick dog. It is better for it to be at home where it will be at ease, if this is possible, and you, the owner, will be the one person who can help to provide the will the spaniel needs to fight the illness. There are unfortunately no guarantees of success, as there are none in serious human illness, but at least you can know that everything possible has been done to help the dog win through. My Springer was a tough dog but he was very ill indeed, and I am convinced that my being with him helped him in his fight; it may have been just enough to tip the scales in his favour.

Less seriously, indigestion sometimes troubles dogs or puppies who have over-eaten; it is usually evidenced by stomach rumblings and a general uneasiness that prevents the dog from settling. A teaspoonful of a mixture of water and Milk of Magnesia is a good remedy but be careful not to give too much – or constipation will result.

Constipation can easily lead to more serious conditions. If it occurs, the reasons need investigating. It may be due to a faulty diet – too much biscuit, for example – but it might be caused by an obstruction, even a growth. If it does not clear up rapidly with the aid of a dessertspoonful of olive oil daily for a few days, veterinary advice is needed. Olive oil, incidentally, is a good laxative for puppies and also helps improve the coat and condition. It is probably best given (a half or one teaspoonful, on food) for conditioning purposes during summer, using cod-liver oil as a winter conditioner.

Cod-liver oil is very good for a spaniel's coat, the dose being about half a teaspoonful for young puppies up to two teaspoonfuls a day for adult spaniels. It is not necessary every day all the year round, but helps improve the coat of an out-of-condition dog and is a good booster if fed say once or twice a week.

Worms

Some indigestion, and a number of other conditions, can be

caused by the presence of worms – roundworms, hookworms or tapeworms. Most dogs and puppies have them at some time or another. The roundworm is the most common of the forms and can often be detected in the faeces of the dog, usually a jellified type of diarrhoea. There are several preparations which can be obtained from a good pet shop or chemist which will clear up roundworm (and hookworm) infections without much trouble. (My dogs take Beecham's Canovel quite readily.) Dosage instructions are given on the packet and depend on the weight of the dog. Give these tablets regularly, say once every two months or so, especially if you are keeping several dogs. Bitches should be dosed after whelping and when the puppies have their first dosing.

Tapeworms are a more difficult problem and again can often be detected in the dog's faeces; sections of the tapeworm appear, looking like grains of rice. The worm may be several feet in length, a nasty parasite in the dog's intestine. They do not appear to be passed from dog to dog and may be acquired through the bite of a flea or other insect. Consult a veterinary surgeon. The presence of a tapeworm will affect your spaniel, the recognisable symptoms being a general listlessness, dull eyes and coat and often an unpleasant smell from breath and body.

Skin Parasites

Among the parasites which attack dogs, the most common are fleas. These can be picked up in grass or from other dogs. They secrete themselves in body crevices and cause the dog to scratch, frequently and obviously. There are several good anti-flea preparations around and the best are those which are put into bathwater. Bathing the dog in an Alugan solution (made by Hoechst, obtainable from chemists) is highly effective, also destroying lice and some ticks (two other particularly nasty parasites). The powder is mixed in a bucket to a creamy solution and poured gradually over the dog's coat while it is in the bath. Keep the solution well clear of the spaniel's eyes, and work it into the coat, especially around the tail and under the armpits. Squeeze the coat as dry as possible without rinsing off the solution and towel the dog dry. Such preparations are fine as a protection against fleas (some dogs

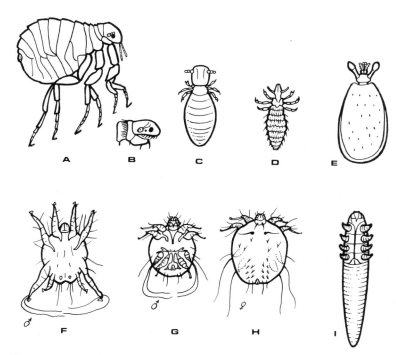

Common external parasites on dogs (many times magnified). A: common flea (human and dog); B: head and mouth of dog flea; C: louse (biting form); D: louse (sucking form); E: blood-sucking tick; F: external ear-mite; G and H: male and female mange mites; I: follicular mange parasite

seem more susceptible to them than others and can lose part of their coat and develop a skin allergy to them) and can be used every few weeks if necessary.

Lice, which are small and grey in colour, cause much irritation, laying eggs and hatching them out on the spaniel's skin in five days.

Ticks, sometimes picked up in sheep fields, are ferocious little parasites that burrow into the flesh of the dog, usually sucking its blood and swelling up to a recognisable size as a result. They should not be pulled out, since their mouth pincers will remain in the dog and set up a site of infection. Dropping a spot of eucalyptus oil or turpentine directly on them usually releases them and they can be destroyed.

Obesity

Obesity is a disorder which should be viewed seriously. Elsewhere in this book I have mentioned that a fat spaniel is not a healthy one. Some spaniels do put on weight in middle age, and although this may be due to a thyroid deficiency – in which case veterinary treatment will be needed – it is more likely to be caused by overeating, eating the wrong food, and/or insufficient exercise. If you have adhered strictly to all the precautions against your spaniel becoming too fat – giving it the right diet and exercise throughout its life – then the cause may be something which needs a veterinary surgeon's diagnosis. If the cause is too much food (or titbits), then all sweet and fatty foodstuffs must be cut out and the dog put on a diet of raw, fresh meat – approximately 30g per kilo (½oz per lb) body weight daily; an egg beaten up with a little milk and brown bread every other day will supplement this diet, and the dog is then weighed every day to see how it is progressing. The best method of weighing your spaniel (the Clumber may be an exception due to its size) is to stand yourself on a set of bathroom scales, note your weight then stand on again holding the dog and note the difference.

Stress

It is worth mentioning stress as a disorder. The word has many interpretations where dogs are concerned, but generally it means anxiety or nervousness caused by environmental conditions or people. A dog can be 'stressed' in many ways and may respond in many ways. It can become nervous, withdrawn or aggressive. It can become physically ill as well as mentally disturbed. If a dog becomes frightened of something, for instance traffic, it should not be subjected to the noise more than is absolutely essential. If it is nervous of gunfire, it will obviously not make a good gundog. Precautions should be taken to avoid the cause of harassment. Teasing, perhaps by your visitors, by children or by passersby, often has a devastating effect on a dog. It may become highly nervous, aggressive or even vicious – and that will *not* be the dog's fault. If a dog's trust is betrayed, the result is a bewildered animal affected by stress, and it will become unstable and probably ill.

Appendix 1
Parts and Points of the Dog

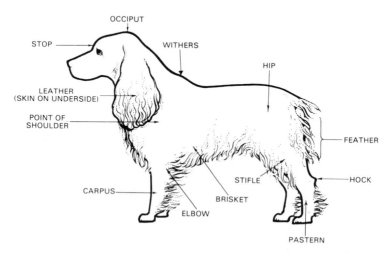

Main points of the spaniel

Apple-head   Rounded or domed, instead of flat-topped head.

Blaze   White markings upwards on the face between the eyes.

Brisket   The body area in front of the chest.

Butterfly nose   Spotted or speckled nose or muzzle.

Cat foot   Short, rounded foot with well-developed high knuckles.

Chest   The body area down from brisket to belly.

Cobby   Short, compact and in proportion.

Dew claw   Extra claw (a vestigial thumb) on the inside of the foreleg; needs to be removed by veterinary surgeon soon after birth.

Dish-faced   Having a nose which is higher than the muzzle at the stop.

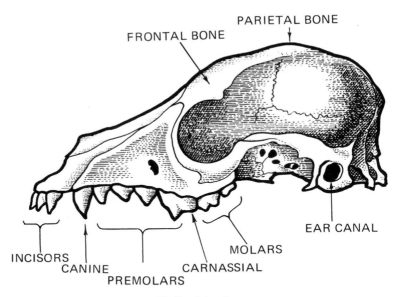

Skull of the dog

Docking Shortening of the tail, carried out soon after birth.

Elbow The joint at the top of the forearm.

Feather The long, fine hair fringes at the back of the legs and under the tail.

Forearm Part of the foreleg extending from elbow to pastern.

Frill A mass of feathery hair on the chest.

Hare foot A long and narrow foot, carried forward.

Haw Red inside eyelid.

Height This is measured at the shoulder with the head bent slightly downwards.

Hocks The hock joints.

Hucklebones The tops of the hip joints.

Knee The joint connecting the forearm and the fore-pastern.

Leather The skin of the ear.

Occiput The slightly projecting bone or bump which appears at the back of the head.

Overshot Having the teeth of the upper jaw projecting beyond those of the lower jaw.

180

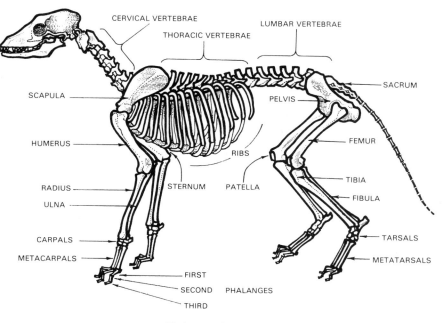

Skeleton of the dog

Pastern The lowest part of the leg, below the knee or hock.

Pily Soft coat.

Septum The division between the nostrils.

Smudge nose A nose which is neither spotted nor entirely black.

Stern Tail.

Stifles The top joints of the hind legs.

Stop Depression at junction of nose and skull.

Undershot Teeth of the lower jaw projecting in front of those of the upper jaw.

Withers Top of the back, above the shoulder.

Appendix 2
Quarantine

No book about dogs can be complete without a reference to rabies and Britain's quarantine laws. If you have travelled abroad with your spaniel, or even bought it overseas, then it must enter quarantine for a period of six months when you bring it into the UK. There are no exceptions, however certain you may be that the dog could not possibly have contracted rabies. This appears hard on the dog, but it is the method that has kept Britain free of an appalling disease.

Quite apart from the quarantine regulations, no dog may be brought into Britain without the owner first obtaining an import licence – from the Import Licence Section, Ministry of Agriculture, Fisheries and Food, Government Buildings, Toby Jug Site, Hook Rise South, Tolworth, Surrey, England.

Appendix 3
Useful Addresses

THE KENNEL CLUB 1 Clarges Street, Piccadilly, London W1Y 8AB. Registration of all pedigree dogs. Information on clubs and associations, breed standards, shows, etc.

AMERICAN KENNEL CLUB 51 Madison Avenue, New York, NY10010, USA. Registration of American pedigree dogs, information on shows, standards of breeds and activities in the USA.

DOG BREEDERS' ASSOCIATES 1 Abbey Road, Bourne End, Bucks SL8 5NZ. Lists of breeders with available puppies – a free service.

ROYAL SOCIETY FOR THE PREVENTION OF CRUELTY TO ANIMALS The Causeway, Horsham, Sussex.

BRITISH FIELD SPORTS SOCIETY 59 Kennington Road, London SE1 7PZ.

AMERICAN SPANIEL CLUB 12 Woodland, Woodmere, New York, NY11598, USA. Information on breed standards, shows and activities relating to spaniels in the USA.

Breed Councils and Societies for Spaniel Breeds in the UK
(Courtesy of the Kennel Club of Great Britain)

COCKER SPANIEL BREED COUNCIL Mr J. W. Bosomworth, 10 Park Square, Leeds LS1 2LM.

DORSET WORKING SPANIEL CLUB Miss A. Harrison, Beacon Hill Cottage, West Morden, Wareham, Dorset.

EASTERN COUNTIES SPANIEL SOCIETY Mrs A. Wentworth-Smith, The Old Rectory, Swardeston, Norwich.

GWYNEDD SPANIEL CLUB Mrs V. M. Davies, Coedfryn, Lower Halkyn, Holywell CH8 8ES.

MID-SUSSEX WORKING SPANIEL CLUB Mrs Newbury, 27 Balaclava Road, Surbiton, Surrey.

NORTH OF ENGLAND SPANIEL CLUB Mrs F. Curran, Glen View, Stannerford Road, Crawcrook, Co Durham.

NORTH WEST ULSTER SPANIEL CLUB Mr S. Lees, 12 Westland Drive, Magherafelt, Co Derry.

SCOTTISH SPANIEL CLUB Mr D. M. Douglas, Frogfield, Laurencekirk, Kincardineshire.

SPANIEL CLUB Mr C. Sutcliffe, Nertherwood Farm, Bromley Wood, Abbots Bromley, Rugeley, Staffs WS15 3AG.

WELSH & ENGLISH COUNTIES SPANIEL CLUB Mrs M. M. Leopard, Lower Kimbilton Farm, Leominster, Hereford.

WESTERN COUNTIES & SOUTH WALES SPANIEL CLUB Mr A. M. Peace, 23 Durleigh Road, Bridgwater, Somerset.

Clubs and Societies for Specific Spaniel Breeds

AMERICAN COCKER

AMERICAN COCKER SPANIEL CLUB OF GREAT BRITAIN Mrs A. M. Jones, The Captains, Castle Morton, Malvern, Worcs.

HOME COUNTIES AMERICAN COCKER CLUB Mrs C. M. Scott, Woodview Cottage, Bridge Lane, Wellington, Herefords.

NORTHERN COUNTIES AMERICAN COCKER SPANIEL CLUB Mrs M. F. Slapp, 2 The Crescent, Broadwater, Fleetwood, Lancs.

BRITTANY

While no Brittany Spaniel club or society has been established in the UK at the time of writing, much information on the breed can be obtained from Mr C. Stanley Smith, Saltwood, 5 Pump Lane, Rainham, Gillingham, Kent, who is also in touch with the Club de L'Epagneul Breton – on whose standards the current UK breed standards are based.

CAVALIER KING CHARLES

CAVALIER KING CHARLES SPANIEL CLUB Mrs D. MacLaine, The Grove, Mundon, Maldon, Essex.

EASTERN COUNTIES CAVALIER KING CHARLES SPANIEL SOCIETY Mrs E. M. J. Tweddell, 45 Parklands Avenue, Shipdham, Thetford, Norfolk.

MIDLAND CAVALIER KING CHARLES SPANIEL CLUB Mrs F. S. Stewart, Leigh Court, near Worcester WR6 5LB.

NORTHERN CAVALIER KING CHARLES SPANIEL SOCIETY Miss B. M. Henshaw, The Orchard, Wharf Lane, Kendal, Cumbria.

NORTHERN IRELAND CAVALIER KING CHARLES SPANIEL CLUB
Mrs B. Megarry, 21 Victoria Road, Ballyhalbert, New-
townards, Co Down.

SCOTTISH CAVALIER KING CHARLES SPANIEL CLUB Mr G.
Donaldson, Viewfield, 122 Main Street, Larbert FK5 3LA.

SOUTH AND WEST CAVALIER KING CHARLES SPANIEL CLUB
Mrs B. Snape, 173 Elan Way, Caldicot, Newport.

SOUTHERN CAVALIER KING CHARLES SPANIEL CLUB Mrs J.
Wright, 198 Connaught Road, Brookwood, Woking,
Surrey.

WEST OF ENGLAND CAVALIER KING CHARLES SPANIEL CLUB
Mrs D. Fry, Tall Timbers, Summers Lane, Knightcott,
Banwell, Avon.

CLUMBER

CLUMBER SPANIEL CLUB Mr G. M. Bryant, Coldharbour
Farm, Glastonbury, Somerset.

COCKER

BLACK COCKER SPANIEL SOCIETY Mr M. Chivers, Whitegates,
Alton Road, Odiham, Basingstoke, Hants.

CHESHIRE COCKER SPANIEL CLUB Mrs N. Curtis, Corner-
ways, London Road, Prestbury, near Macclesfield,
Cheshire.

COCKER SPANIEL CLUB Mr A. E. Simpson, Coltrim, 33
Engayne Gardens, Upminster, Essex RM14 1UY.

COCKER SPANIEL CLUB OF LANCASHIRE Mrs D. M. Schofield,
Cobbles, Norcott Brook, near Warrington, Cheshire WA4
4DX.

COCKER SPANIEL CLUB OF SCOTLAND Mr and Mrs A.
Crichton, 12 The Crescent, Longriggend, near Airdrie
ML6 7TR.

COVENTRY COCKER SPANIEL CLUB Mrs M. Allard, 49 Angela
Ave, Potters Green, Coventry CV2 2GH.

DEVON AND CORNWALL COCKER SPANIEL CLUB Mr. M. Owens,
299 Fort Austin Avenue, Crownhill, Plymouth PL6 5TQ

EAST ANGLIAN COCKER SPANIEL SOCIETY Mrs O. B. Norfolk,
'Tarlings', West Hanningfield, Essex CM2 8UU.

EAST OF SCOTLAND COCKER SPANIEL CLUB Mrs E. Johnston,
Knocktower, Newbridge, Midlothian.

HOME COUNTIES COCKER CLUB   D. J. Telford, 39 Spencer Road, Benfleet, Essex.

LONDON COCKER SPANIEL SOCIETY   Mr R. W. Crisp, Layhanm, 84 Wembley Hill Road, Wembley, Middx.

MIDLAND COCKER SPANIEL CLUB   Mr R. M. A. Pain, 57 New Inns Lane, Rubery, Worcs.

NORTH MIDLANDS AND EASTERN COUNTIES COCKER SPANIEL CLUB   Mrs W. M. Price, Church Farm, The Green, Findern, Derby.

NORTH OF ENGLAND COCKER SPANIEL CLUB   Mrs R. Tyson, 'Browster', 71 Egerton Road South, Chorlton, Manchester M21 1XH.

NORTH OF IRELAND COCKER SPANIEL CLUB   Mr T. J. Gracey, 67 Knockvale Park, Belfast.

NORTH WALES COCKER SPANIEL CLUB   Mr D. Gorse, 2 Gorder Mynydd, Gwenymynyod, Mold, Clwyd CH7 4AD.

PARTI-COLOUR COCKER SPANIEL CLUB   Mr W. R. Blythe, Lincoln Flats Kennels, Foggathorpe, near Selby, Humberside YO8 7PZ.

RED AND GOLDEN COCKER SPANIEL CLUB   Mr A. Hempstead, 2 Barrow Green Road, Oxted, Surrey.

ROTHERHAM AND DISTRICT COCKER SPANIEL CLUB   Mr W. R. Blythe, Lincoln Flats Kennels, Foggathorpe, near Selby, Humberside YO8 7PZ.

SOUTH WALES AND MONMOUTHSHIRE COCKER SPANIEL CLUB   Mrs T. M. Bebb, Bona Vista, 148 Cefn Road, Rogerstone, Gwent NP1 9EX.

ULSTER COCKER SPANIEL CLUB   Mr T. J. Cardy, Mount Keepe, 36 Glen Road, Lower Castlereagh, Belfast.

WEST OF ENGLAND COCKER SPANIEL CLUB   Mr W. K. Price, 'Bienvenu', Parkend Road, Coalway, Coleford, Glos.

YORKSHIRE COCKER SPANIEL CLUB   Mr E. Walker, 53 Westwick Road, Sheffield 8.

ENGLISH SPRINGER

ANTRIM AND DOWN ENGLISH SPRINGER SPANIEL CLUB   Mr N. Graham, 15 The Glade, Mossley, Newtownabbey, N. Ireland.

ENGLISH SPRINGER SPANIEL CLUB   Mrs J. Wood, Ashorne Hill Farm, Ashorne, Warwick.

ENGLISH SPRINGER SPANIEL CLUB OF NORTHERN IRELAND   Mr E. Wilson, 30 Glenavy Road, Lisburn, Co Antrim.

ENGLISH SPRINGER CLUB OF SCOTLAND   Mrs E. K. Thomson, Rivington Lodge, Castle Douglas, Scotland.

ENGLISH SPRINGER SPANIEL CLUB OF WALES   Mr M. Shefford, Pal Mawr, Felindre, Near Swansea.

MIDLAND ENGLISH SPRINGER SPANIEL SOCIETY   Mrs M. Backhouse, 121 Silcoates Lane, Wrenthorpe, near Wakefield, Yorks.

NORTHERN ENGLISH SPRINGER SPANIEL SOCIETY   Mrs E. Dobson, Teesview Gundogs, Neasham, Co Durham.

SOUTHERN ENGLISH SPRINGER SPANIEL CLUB   Mr D. Miller, Beacon View Boarding Kennels, St Leonard Road, Chivery, near Tring, Herts.

FIELD

FIELD SPANIEL SOCIETY   Mr R. Hall Jones, The Captains, Castle Morton, Malvern, Worcs.

IRISH WATER

IRISH WATER SPANIEL ASSOCIATION   Mrs J. Johnson, Coinros, Clements End, Coleford, Glos.

KING CHARLES

KING CHARLES SPANIEL ASSOCIATION   Mrs G. M. Simpson, 'Annanfield', 5 Stefan Close, Hooe, Plymouth PL9 9RS.

KING CHARLES SPANIEL CLUB   Mr. N. Beck, 208 Bromley Road, Beckenham, Kent.

NORTHERN KING CHARLES SPANIEL CLUB   Mrs S. Taylor, 12 Duxbury Avenue, Little Lever, Bolton, Lancs BL3 1PX.

PAPILLONS

PAPILLON (BUTTERFLY DOG) CLUB   Mr M. W. Hutchings, Gerlil, Cherry Tree Road, Milford, Godalming, Surrey.

PAPILLON (BUTTERFLY DOG) CLUB OF SCOTLAND   Mrs A. McKnight, The Cairns, Charleston, Nigg, Aberdeen.

SOUTH WALES PAPILLON CLUB   Mrs V. Hughes, 42 Dinas Street, Plasmare, City of Swansea.

SUSSEX

SUSSEX SPANIEL ASSOCIATION   Mrs Lancaster, Moss Cottage, (Nursery Rd) Glos Lane, Alsager, Stoke-on-Trent, Staffs.

TIBETAN

NORTHERN TIBETAN SPANIEL CLUB   Mrs D. Charlton, Stone Riggs, Great Smeaton, Northallerton, N. Yorks.

SOUTH WESTERN TIBETAN SPANIEL CLUB   Mrs D. Jenkins, Amcross Cottage, Ashton Keynes, Swindon, Wilts SN6 6NT.

TIBETAN SPANIEL ASSOCIATION   Mrs K. Tomlinson, 'Pasuanto', Buxted, Uckfield, Sussex TN22 4JU.

WELSH SPRINGER

WELSH SPRINGER SPANIEL CLUB   Mrs A. M. Walton, Hill Park Farm, Wrotham, Sevenoaks, Kent.

WELSH SPRINGER SPANIEL CLUB OF SOUTH WALES   Mrs P. Sherwin, Ash Tree Lodge, Mathern, Chepstow, Gwent.

Note: Full lists of canine societies, training clubs and field trial societies, and information on relevant activities, can be obtained in the UK from the Kennel Club, and in the USA from either the American Kennel Club or the American Spaniel Club (addresses above).

Acknowledgements

My very grateful thanks are due to my patient spaniels, Gipsy and Joanna, who have joined in my work and watched with interest the progress of this book, firmly reminding me when it was time for games, walks or dinners – or just when they wanted attention.

Thanks in large measure are due to many breeders and owners, and others who so obviously care about spaniels, for lending me their dogs to be photographed, and for giving up their time and helping with old records and advice, as well as guiding me around the tricky areas of the show-ring. In particular I should like to mention Jane Lilley, Ann Findlay and Mr & Mrs J. S. Walton, who have been especially helpful, and indeed all their jolly spaniels.

I owe a debt of gratitude, too, to Keith Cardwell who very ably and professionally carried out the photography for this book. I am sure he did not realise just what he was in for when he agreed to photograph so many dogs for me. His patience in travelling into the depths of the countryside, with long-suffering hours spent in all weathers, a wide variety of working conditions and contorted positions, will be gratefully remembered.

My thanks are also inevitably due to my wife Valerie, who lost sleep, company and conversation over my work; to Debbie Baker and Shirley Phillips who patiently typed and retyped the manuscripts, suffering my many alterations and additional notes without audible sighs; to G. Roland Smith for patience and professionalism in producing the drawings for the book – many of which were interpreted with great flair from weird scribbles of my own – and last, but most certainly not least, to Kay Reynolds who, at 15 years of age, very bravely saved the life of my precious spaniel Gipsy.

Index

Figures in italic indicate illustrations

Adult spaniels, 60–1
Alpine spaniels, 12, 35
American Cocker spaniel, 17, 49, 52–3, 123–6, *52*
  Kennel Club, 50, 51, 53, 122
  Spaniels, 50–5, *54 see also* American Cocker Spaniel, American Water Spaniel and Springer Spaniel, American
  Spaniel Club, 122
  Water Spaniel, 49, 50, 51, *52*
Anal irritation, 98
Arkwright, William, 16, 35
Arthritis, 170–1
Artificial respiration, 157

Balls, 65, 158
Bandaging, 153
Barbet, 15
Basket, 64, 71
Bathing, 95–6, 176
Berners, Dame Juliana, 10
Black spaniel, 26–7
Blenheim spaniel, 14, 44, 46–8
Blindness, 18
Bones, feeding, 85
Bowers, 38
Bowl, feeding, 64, 84, *65*
Breech birth, 76
Breed Standards, 123–44
Breton spaniel, 31, 36, 49 *see also* Brittany spaniel
Brittany spaniel, 17, 31–3, 36, 51–2, 59, 127–8, 145, *32, 103*
Broken limbs, 156
Brown Water spaniel *see* American Water spaniel
Brushes, 65, 93, 120
Brushing, 70, 93, 95
Burns and scalds, 156–7
Butterfly spaniel *see* Papillon

Caesarian, 76

Caius, Dr John, 10, 12, 48
Canker, 99, 168
Car sickness *see* Travelling
Castration, 100–1
Cavalier King Charles spaniel, 14, 17, 43, 46–8, 57, 129–30, *47, 118*
Charcoal, 160
Chaucer, Geoffrey, 9
Check chain, 105
Checks, medical, 98–9
Children, playing with, 68, 72
Choking, 158
Classes, 116, 122
Clipping, 96
Clumber spaniel, 12, 16, 17, 33–6, 52, 57, 59, 130–1, 178, *33, 58, 90*
Coat polishers, 91
Cocker spaniel, 14, 16, 17, 18, 19–21, 23, 25, 26, 27, 39, 53, 56–7, 59, 61, 68, 73, 86, 87, 91, 93, 119, 131–2, 149, 150, 167, *19, 21, 112, 118*
Cocker Spaniel Field Trial Club (USA), 52
Cod-liver oil, 175
Collars, 65, 105
Combs, 95, 97
Comforter, 10, 45, 46
Commands, 69, 106, 147
Conjunctivitis, 169
Constipation, 175
Continental Toy Spaniel, 43 *see also* Papillon
Coughs, 172
Countryside, training for, 111–14
Cow's milk, 79, 81
Cox, Nicholas, 13
Cruft, Charles, 121
Cruft's Dog Show, 56, 116, 117, 121
Cuvier, Georges, 12, 35
Cystitis, 171

Daniel, 34
Dew claws, 78

Diabetes, 171
Diet, 63, 65, 67, 68, 78, 82, 83, 87, 99,
    170, 173, 174, 178
Digestive disorders, 173-5
Distemper, 68, 172
Dobson, William, 14
Docking tails, 78
Drowning, 157
Dry baths, 97
Dutch spaniels, 49-50
Dwarf spaniel, 42 *see also* Papillon

Ears, 95-6, 99, 167-9
Ectropion, 169
Edwards, Sydenham, 14
Electric shock, 157
Elderly spaniels, care of, 96, 99, 170
Elizabethan collar, 155, 172, *155*
English Cocker Spaniel Club of
    America, 53
    Cocker spaniel (USA), 53
    Springer spaniel *see* Springer spaniel,
        English
    Springer Spaniel Trial Association
        (USA), 53
    Toy spaniel, 46
    Water spaniel, 48
Entering a show, 115-17
Entropion, 169
Eucalyptus oil, 95, 160, 161, 177
Evelyn, John, 10
Eye drops, 169
Eyes, 95-6, 99, 169-70

False heat, 74; pregnancy, 74
Farmstock, 113
Feeding, 83-7
Field spaniel, 17, 26, 27, 39-40, 54, 57,
    59, 134-6, *39*
Field trials, 116, 120-1
Fights, 154
First-aid box, 160-2
Fleas, 176, 177
French spaniels, 49
Friesian Curly, 50
Fungal infections, 171-2

Gestation, 75
Gin traps, 91
Goat's milk, 79
Grass seeds, 168
Grooming, 92-5
Grouse, 150

Gunfire training, 149

Haemorrhagic gastroenteritis, 110, 174
Hard pad, 68
Hay fever, 172
Heart conditions, 172
Heat exhaustion, 72, 157-8
Heat in bitches *see* Season
Herbal remedies, 160
Honey, 161
Household cleaning agents, poisoning
    by, 159
House training, 69, 104-5
Hunting up, 147
Hysterectomy, 100, 173

Indigestion, 175
Inoculation, 68
Interbreeding, 73
Irish Water spaniel, 15, 17, 27-31, 49,
    54, 57, 59, 78, 109, 136-7, 150, *29,
    30*

Jacobs, Thomas, 27
Jumping up, 108-9

Kennel Club, 16-17, 54, 59, 63, 97, 115,
    121, 122
Kennel cough, 172
King Charles spaniel, 10, 14, 17, 26,
    43-6, 57, 137-8, *44*

Labour, 76
Langdale, A. W., 35
Leads, 65, 105
Lead training, 105-6
Leptospirosis, 68
Lice, 176, 177
Lifting, 92
Linnaeus, 12

Market-stall selling, 59
Marrow, 85
Mating, 74
McCarthy, Justin, 28
Medicine, administering, 164-7, *165*
Metritis, 173
Milk, 78, 79; excess in bitches, 78-9;
    substitute, 80-1
Mites, 177
Morrison, Mrs McLaren, 41
Muzzling, 154, *154*

Nails, 98

Nervousness, 88, 92, 178
Norfolk spaniel, 48-9
Northern Ireland Water spaniel, 49

Obedience championships, 121
Obesity, 178 *see* Diet
Old English spaniel, 48
Olive oil, 175

Pain relievers, 161
Papillon, 17, 42-3, 57, 138-40, *43*
Parasites, 93, 176-7, *177*
Partridge, 150
Parts and points of the dog, 179-81, *179*
Pedigree, 53, 163
Pepys, Samuel, 13
Pheasant, 150
Picard spaniel, 49
Placenta, 77, 173
Play, 69
Poisoning, 158-60
Pont Audemer spaniel, 49
Pregnancy, 76
Preparation (for a show), 117-20
Pulse, 167
Puppy, selecting a, 62-3; feeding, 65-8, 80-2; training, 69-71
Pyometra, 173

Quarantine, 182
Quartering, 149

Rearing by hand, 79
Respiratory and heart conditions, 172-3
Retrieving, 147-50
Rosehill kennels, 37
Roundworms, 176

Salivation, 98
Scalds, 156
Scaling teeth, 170
Scottish spaniel, 49
Season, 74
Shampoos, 95, 162
Sheep worrying, 113
Showing colour, 74
Show ring equipment, 120
Shows, 115, 116, 120-2
Skidmore, 28
Skin parasites *see* Parasites
Sleep, 70
Slimming, 86

Snakebites, 155
Snipe, 150
Spaying, 100, 170
Springer spaniel, American, 53
    English, 14, 17, 21-6, 35, 39, 48, 53, 59, 60, 70, 87, 109, 132-4, 149, 152, *22, 94, 146, 148*
    Welsh, 14, 17, 21-6, 27, 35, 39, 48, 53-4, 57, 59, 70, 91, 143-4, 149, *24, 81*
Squirrel dog, 42 *see also* Papillon
Stings, 161
Stress, 92, 110, 178
Stud dog, 74, 75
Sulphur, 86, 160
Sussex spaniel, 17, 26, 27, 35, 36-8, 55, 57, 59, 140-1, *37, 66*
Syringe feeding, 80

Tapeworms, 176
Taplin, W., 14
Teeth, 98-9, 170
Temperature, 76, 78, 79, 163, 167
Tibetan spaniel, 17, 26, 40-2, 57, 142-3, *40, 58*
Ticks, 176, 177
Toys, 65, 68
Travelling, 71, 117
Travelling cage, 117, 120
Tricks, 111
Trimming, 96-7
Tumours, 100, 170
Tweed Irish Water spaniel, 28

Umbilical cord, 77
Uterine sepsis, 77

Vaccination, 63 *see also* Inoculation
Vasectomy, 101
Viral hepatitis, 68
Vitamins in pregnancy, 76

Water bag, 76
Water, drinking, 85
Welsh Springer spaniel *see* Springer spaniel, Welsh
Whelping, 75-8; boxes, 75; calendar, 75
White, John, 41
Working spaniel, training a, 146-50
Working trials, 120-1
Worming, 63, 65, 68, 162, 176
Wounds, 153-5

Youatt, 38, 48